A Hitting Clinic:
The Walt Hriniak Way

By Walt Hriniak

With Henry Horenstein and Mark Starr

A Pond Press Book

PERENNIAL LIBRARY

Harper & Row, Publishers, New York
Cambridge, Philadelphia, San Francisco, Washington
London, Mexico City, São Paulo, Singapore, Sydney

Front cover photograph: Peter Travers
Back cover photograph: Henry Horenstein

Production: Pond Press/Henry Horenstein
Editor: Lauren Lantos
Art Direction/Design: DeFrancis Studio
Mechanicals: John Colan
Picture Research: Stephanie Yoffee
Copyediting and Proofreading: Diane Taraskiewicz
    and Donna Gordon

FIRST EDITION

LIBRARY OF CONGRESS CATALOG CARD NUMBER: 87-45626
ISBN: 0-06-096226-7 (pbk.)

88 89 90 91 92   10 9 8 7 6 5 4 3 2 1

This book is dedicated to my mother and father and to my daughter, Jill.

A Hitting Clinic: The Walt Hriniak Way

Table of Contents

Acknowledgments

The authors would like to thank John Carroll, athletic director at Natick High School, for getting us together to write this book, and Dan Bial, our editor, for his enthusiasm and patience. Several players gave us a lot of help: in particular, Wade Boggs and Dwight Evans of the Boston Red Sox, and Carney Lansford of the Oakland Athletics. Thanks also to the entire Boston Red Sox organization.

Charles Miller, of Massachusetts Institute of Technology, did an outstanding job with his high-speed photographs, as did Glenn Reid, with his line illustrations. Thanks also to all the photographers who submitted work for the book, especially Peter Travers. These photographs are credited in the back of the book.

Several other individuals and organizations helped with various parts of the project, especially Pat Kelly of the National Baseball Library, Cooperstown, N.Y., and Noreen O'Gara of the Boston Public Library. And thanks to Ed Braverman, Michael Carey, Karen Cogan, Elise Katz, Debbie Matson, and Jean O'Connell for their help.

Sometimes I feel as if I was born swinging a bat. But I guess I didn't begin hitting in earnest until I was five years old. Once I started, though, I never stopped. Baseball was a marathon game for me. As a kid growing up in Tampa, Florida, I'd get up in the morning around eight and race to a vacant lot, where my buddies and I would play until it was too dark to see. We'd play three on a side, and in a few weeks I'd get a season's worth of at-bats.

I knew I had a lot of natural ability, but I didn't take hitting for granted. I kept playing and playing and hitting and hitting. When I wasn't outside swinging a bat, I was swinging whatever was handy—brooms, tennis racquets, whatever. I just kept swinging. It went on that way through Little League, Senior League, and American Legion ball until I was signed by the Red Sox.

Before I became a pro, my main teacher was my dad. He had played softball in the Air Force for 25 seasons. He knew a lot about hitting, and he drilled two fundamentals into me: WAIT and WEIGHT. Wait on the ball, and then transfer your weight while swinging. I accepted that philosophy and still apply it.

I first met Walt Hriniak in the Instructional League back in 1977, but we didn't have our first real talk until spring training in 1982. We found we had a lot in common. My "wait and weight" hitting style was basically in accordance with Walt's own theories. We also shared the attitude that constructing a swing was kind of like building a house. You have to lay a good foundation before you can build.

That's what is so incredible about Walt. He examines your swing from the feet up and puts you under a microscope. A lot of people who discuss or coach hitting really don't get beyond the swing. They concentrate all their attention on how the bat moves through the strike zone. To Walt, the swing is just one facet of hitting a baseball. He watches the feet, the legs, the hands—everything that goes together to produce a swing.

Walt is living proof that you don't have to be a Hall of Famer to teach hitting. You have to be able to communicate, and that's where Walt excels. We share another philosophy about learning to hit: Don't just swing to swing. Practice as if you are playing in a real game. You know the old adage—"practice makes perfect." For Walt and me, it runs, "practice doesn't make perfect; perfect practice makes perfect."

The first time Walt and I really worked together was spring training of 1982. That year, playing in 104 games, I hit .349. But I had only 338 at-bats, not enough to qualify for the batting title, which Willie Wilson won hitting .332. The next year I found myself the regular Red Sox third baseman, and I also won my first batting crown with a .361 average.

Wade Boggs

From the very start of spring training to the last day each season, Walt and I are constant companions. I never thought I would find someone as interested in hitting as I am, but Walt is surely my equal. We talk about hitting all the time—before games, in the dugout, wherever. We talk about my swing, the opposing pitcher, the ballpark we're playing in, and anything else that might affect me at the plate on that particular day. Walt knows my swing so well that he can immediately pinpoint any problems I'm having. The quick feedback enables me to make a correction the very next time I come to bat.

After winning my second batting crown in 1985, I told the audience at a Red Sox awards banquet, "I can't express what Walt has meant to me and my baseball career, but I'll say that I've got so much from Walt that I can't give back. Certainly my winning batting titles is a reflection on him." Several years and several batting titles later, I still feel the same way.

Ever watch golf? Some scrawny guy, no bigger than five-foot-five, 140 pounds, steps up to the tee and whacks the ball 300 yards. Then some weightlifter stomps up to the tee and is lucky to dribble the ball 150 yards. Yet nobody is really surprised. We accept that driving a golf ball successfully requires a lot more than strength.

The same is true of hitting a baseball. But not until very recently did people really understand exactly what hitting involves. This is partly because baseball has developed far more mystique, I believe, than any other sport. And most of that mystique has been applied to a single skill—hitting a baseball. That's why great pitchers such as Cy Young, Christy Mathewson, and Sandy Koufax are mere Hall of Famers, while great hitters such as Babe Ruth,

To fans, great hitters such as Babe Ruth and Ted Williams are legends, while great pitchers are mere Hall of Famers.

Joe DiMaggio, and Ted Williams are legends. Nobody ever tells stories about Cy Young calling a strikeout the way they do about Babe Ruth calling his home-run shot. Nobody ever wrote a story about Sandy Koufax's last strikeout like they did about Ted Williams's last home run. Nobody ever wrote a song that went, "Where have you gone, Christy Mathewson?"

A lot of people say that hitting a baseball is the single most difficult task in all sports. I don't disagree. You also hear people talk about the "art" of hitting. I *do* disagree with that. Hitting is a science. However, it's a brand-new science, one that we've been studying with modern tools for only a little more than a decade.

As far as I'm concerned, the real pioneer of this science was the late Charlie Lau. Charlie was a catcher who spent eleven years in the majors with four different clubs, then went on to become hitting coach for the Kansas City Royals, the New York Yankees, and the Chicago White Sox. He was the first coach to really analyze hitting and break it down into all its components. He used videotape to reveal the secrets of the swing. He discovered that a lot of what was commonly held to be true about hitting simply wasn't true.

When you challenge the established truth, you take a lot of heat. So Charlie's theories came in for criticism from a lot of people—among them some of the game's great hitters. But that didn't deter Charlie. Although he listened to what all the other experts and all the famous hitters had to say, he never

Charlie Lau was a great coach and my close friend.

changed his mind. He believed what he saw with his own eyes, not what he heard from others.

I am a disciple of Charlie Lau. He was my coach, and he later became my very dear friend. I spent some time with Charlie in Florida shortly before he died. We talked about a lot of things, and, of course, we talked about hitting. I told him, "Charlie, I believe in your theories as much as you do. I'm not telling you that because you're my friend. It's because you're right."

I still believe in Charlie's theories. But I didn't come to my conclusions easily or simply out of loyalty. Like almost everyone else, I was skeptical about the "hitting truths" that Charlie was trying to instill in people. I questioned him, challenged him, analyzed each step in my mind, and checked out every aspect of his theories by studying hitters both in person and on videotape. Every time, I'd wind up calling Charlie and admitting that he was right.

I've spent a lot of years working with his theories, refining them and adding my own wrinkles. After all this time, I know that the things I try to teach hitters will work. I believe I can make anyone a better hitter. I can teach hitters how to have a more efficient swing and how to cut down on mistakes. That is my central goal.

Unfortunately, teaching hitting isn't simply a matter of imparting knowledge to a hitter. He has to take that knowledge and combine it with good work habits, dedication, and a commitment to becoming a better hitter. Of course, hitters are interested only in results. I know I can get them those results— but not until they dedicate themselves to working hard at what I teach. Until I can get the player to believe in what I teach him as much as I do—just as Charlie got me to believe in it as much as he did—it's never going to work as well for him as it should.

A lot of hitters, young and old, aren't willing to make that commitment. I tell them when they come to me, "If you want to find out if my theories work or not, fine. But you've got to be willing to work really hard. If you're just going to try it out for a couple of days, then discard it and try something else, it's a waste of our time. There's only one way to find out if it will work for you. That's to put it to use every day in the same way."

I know that what I'm asking of these hitters is pretty scary. I'm asking them to try things they've never tried before, to give up habits that have worked well enough to get them a job in professional baseball. I'm prodding them to leave the head down longer than they've ever done before, or to release the top hand from the bat at a certain point in the swing. They must add new things to their swing and take some old things away. I warn them that

there will be some real ups and downs for a while. I warn them that it's going to be a prolonged struggle.

You can't master hitting overnight, or even in a month. You can only learn pieces of it at a time. And you never stop learning. When things begin to go wrong and a hitter is slumping, it's easy for him to shoot off in a thousand different directions looking for a new stance, a new swing, a new cure for his hitting woes. That's the way Dwight Evans used to be. He called himself "The Man of a Thousand Stances." He had one for every occasion. When things went wrong, he'd discard that stance and try out a new one. No longer. Once he made up his mind he was going to stick to my methods, it eliminated all the guesswork. Dwight has developed into one of the game's outstanding hitters. We always knew what to work on.

I've already told you that I think hitting a baseball is the most difficult task in sports. Now I'm going to amend that a bit. *Coaching* hitting is even more difficult. That's because what I'm preaching is a ritual of incredible tedium. I'm telling the hitter to work relentlessly at doing the same things exactly the same way every single time he takes the bat in his hands—whether it's batting practice in spring training or the seventh game of the World Series.

This means that the hitter's attitude is as critical as his physical skills. He has to have incredible discipline and be willing to make an extraordinary commitment. That part is not fun. The fun comes in the results. Ask Dwight Evans if it was more fun to have 1,000 stances and hit .240 or to have just one stance and hit .300. It's nice having three days off in the middle of the season to rest and relax, maybe go down to Cape Cod or up to Maine. But I'm pretty sure Dwight preferred spending his summer break playing in the All-Star Game. One stance, several All-Star Game hits.

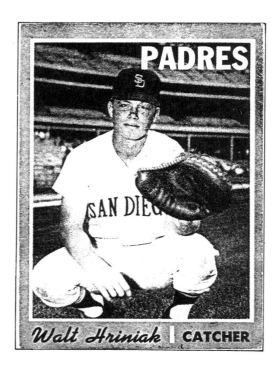

Here I am, the future hitting coach, behind the plate.

Walt Hriniak | CATCHER

I can't hide the fact that I didn't have much of a major-league career. I made it to the big leagues in 1968 at age 25, as a backup catcher with the Atlanta Braves. The following year I ended my stay in the majors in San Diego with the Padres. I guess part of two seasons is a little more than the proverbial cup of coffee in the major leagues—more like a pot of coffee. In all, I played in 47 games and officially went to the plate 99 times. I had 25 hits, all of them singles, making my career batting average .253. I scored four runs and knocked in four runs.

Why should anyone listen to what Walt Hriniak has to say about hitting when he obviously wasn't a great hitter himself? Let me answer by saying that over the years the best managers and coaches in the game generally have been those to whom the game didn't come all that easily. Sparky Anderson lasted one season with the Phillies and hit .218; Tommy Lasorda pitched in 26 games over three seasons and never won a big-league game. Earl Weaver never even made it into the majors. Neither did John McNamara. Many other highly regarded managers—Dick Williams, Tony LaRussa, Whitey Herzog, Gene Mauch, and Chuck Tanner—were strictly journeyman ballplayers. Even though Davey Johnson and Lou Piniella had some fine seasons, neither was blessed with overwhelming talent. They worked very hard to accomplish as much as they did. The only true star managing in the majors today is Pete Rose, and he worked harder as a ballplayer than anyone I've ever seen.

Hitting coaches follow the same trend. Charlie Lau, who was certainly the most noted and respected hitting coach of the modern era, had a long big-league career, but nobody ever mistook him for Mickey Mantle at the plate. In 11 seasons, he had a lifetime average of .255 and hit just 16 home runs. Still, he was the best there was when it came to teaching others how to hit. Those of us to whom it didn't come easily spent a lot more time studying the game and trying to figure it out. We also tend to have more patience with ballplayers who find the secrets of hitting as elusive as we did when we were playing.

In my 10-year career with the Boston Red Sox, I have been fortunate to work with some truly great hitters. Carl Yastrzemski. Carney Lansford. Mike Easler. Dwight Evans. Carlton Fisk. Bill Buckner. Don Baylor. Marty Barrett. Fred Lynn. And, of course, Wade Boggs, the man who currently ranks fourth in career batting average behind immortals Ty Cobb, Rogers Hornsby, and Shoeless Joe Jackson. That's a pretty fair country lineup. It includes a couple of certain Hall of Famers, three former MVPs, five different guys who've won 10 batting crowns among them, and a host of .300 seasons. I am honored that such outstanding ballplayers listened to me and trusted my advice.

I grew up in the suburbs of Boston, and the Red Sox were my favorite team. From the time I was eight years old, I had one dream: to become a major-league baseball player, hopefully with the Bosox. I'm sure I must have done a lot of things as a kid—even gone to school—but all I can remember doing as a youngster was hitting a baseball. Friends remind me I was all-state in football and hockey, too, but baseball was my first love. I was obsessed with hitting. We played games all the time, and when there wasn't a game, we threw batting practice to each other. After dark, we'd play by streetlight. If we didn't have a ball, we'd use paper cups or rocks. We kept hitting until our hands were calloused, like men who perform the hardest manual labor.

My father, Walter Sr., would take me to the park every day and throw batting practice to me. He would talk to me about hitting, but he never made a big deal out of it. And he never, ever yelled at me. If I yelled or acted up, the game was over for the day. "If you're gonna play," he always said to me, "you're gonna play right." He didn't believe in putting too much pressure on kids. He came to all my games in every sport, but I never saw him or heard him. After the game was over, we'd talk quietly about what I did that day and what lessons I learned. I remember one he taught me about how to handle adversity in the field: NEVER make a big deal out of an error. He counseled me to pick up a pebble and throw it away, smooth the dirt around me—and get ready for the next one.

I guess I worked hard at becoming a ballplayer, but I don't remember it as hard work. All I remember is having a lot of fun. That's one of my pet peeves about the way youngsters are taught the game today. They get too much coaching too early. I think they ought to be allowed to just hit and field and not have so much pressure put on them. Besides, so much of what they're taught is either technically wrong or incomplete. How many times have you heard Little League managers yelling to a hitter, "Keep your eye on the ball?" But they seldom tell him exactly how to do that. Also, I wouldn't let kids pitch at all; their arms aren't mature enough for all that stress. Besides, most young pitchers are wild. They don't give young hitters the chance to stand up there and take good strokes. The Little League game is too many walks and too many strikeouts, when it should be hitting and fielding, the two most essential skills in the game. Let the coaches do the pitching. They can throw nice, straight pitches and let the kids spend time developing fundamental skills.

But I'm getting away from my story. I dreamed of being a major leaguer, and when the Milwaukee Braves signed me out of Natick High School for $80,000, a pretty hefty sum in those days, I figured I had it made. Things didn't exactly turn out as I had hoped. Still, today I can look back and say I did make it. I'm proud of each of my 25 hits. But the most important thing to happen to me in baseball happened to me in the minors—on my way up—and I didn't even realize it at the time. I spent nine years in the minors as a second baseman, shortstop, and utility man. In 1968 the Braves organization decided to switch me to catcher. They sent me to their farm club in Shreveport, Louisiana, to play for a rookie manager who had been a catcher for 11 seasons in the majors. That manager was Charlie Lau.

Charlie was only in his mid-thirties, and didn't have the knowledge of hitting that he would a few years later. Nor had he yet developed any new theories on hitting. If he had, he might have made a better hitter out of me, and I might have lasted a bit longer in the big leagues. But even so, Charlie was a natural. He helped me improve my hitting enough to get me up to Atlanta at the end of that year.

Charlie gave me a lot of ideas in that one season that have stayed with me ever since. He really cared about what he was doing, and he was willing to do whatever he could to help his players become better hitters. Charlie reminded me of John Carroll, my wonderful coach at Natick High. The two of them taught me a lot about dedication. They believed in hard work and discipline—for them and for their players. They were always there for me.

I've tried to carry that philosophy into my coaching. I believe in making a total commitment to a hitter, and I hope to get that in return. I'm not just there when the going's good. I'll be there every step of the way, whenever

he needs me. With some players, like Carl Yastrzemski, that meant tele-phone calls in the middle of the night. He'd ask, "What about this idea for a stance?" I never minded those late-night calls.

Charlie taught me how to practice and how to get the most out of myself. His influence started in spring training the very first time he saw me hit. When I was finished in the batting cage, I stepped out, turned to him and said, "Pretty good, huh?" He said, "Well, if I was playing against you, I'd sure know where to play you." I couldn't believe his answer. I thought I'd hit the ball really well, and I was sure he'd be impressed.

Charlie was planting the seeds for dramatic changes in my hitting style and philosophy. For the previous four or five seasons, I'd pretty much tried to

Here I am in my younger days with my fine high school coach, John Carroll, when I played for Natick High School.

pull everything. The Braves had projected me as a power hitter, so I was happy to wind up hitting a respectable .260 or .270 as long as I showed a glimmer of power with double-figure homers. Charlie drummed into me the notion that I should get the most out of my ability and stop trying to be something I wasn't. Maximize your strengths and become the best hitter that you can be, he instructed me. For me, that meant giving up the fantasy of being a home-run hitter. I developed a new philosophy that has guided me ever since. I worked on my mechanics, tried to minimize mistakes, and concentrated on putting the ball in play. Once you put the ball in play, there's always the chance something good will happen. My home runs dropped to three or four that season, but my average jumped to about .300.

But this improvement wasn't enough to carve out a niche in the majors. After I was released in 1971, I was despondent. About three weeks later, I got a call from the first manager I'd ever played for, Jim Fanning, who was then with the Montreal Expos. "Why didn't you call me?" he asked. "Do you still want to play?" I was having a problem with one of my fingers and told him so, but he said, "Come on up to Montreal and we'll talk about it." I got myself up there pretty quickly, and finished up the season catching for Winnipeg, the Expos' Triple-A farm club.

It turned out the Expos were thinking about me more as a coach or manager than as a player. I told them I wasn't sure I could manage, but they insisted that I had an aptitude for it. For the first month of 1972 they started me out as a player-coach in Quebec City. By summer, I found myself manager of the Jamestown, New York, team in the New York-Pennsylvania Rookie League. I'll always be indebted to the Expos for giving me a second chance in baseball. My career as a player was over, but suddenly I found myself with a whole new life in baseball. Yet all I knew about managing was to do things the way I had when I played—with hard work, dedication, and total commitment.

I really enjoyed working with those young kids in Jamestown, which sounds pretty funny because I was just 29 at the time. But they took to my philosophy, which was to play hard. I believed that if we could get the players to play all-out all the time, then they would achieve their full potential. That was all you could really ask of them. Work hard, and the rest would take care of itself. That may sound pretty basic, but it works. After a couple of years as player-coach at the Triple-A level and managing at Jamestown, I was supposed to take over as manager of the Expos' farm team in West Palm Beach. But that year, 1974, the Expos invited me to spring training for the first time. What a thrill to be back in a big-league camp after about five years. The Expos wanted me around because I was a hard worker and willing to throw a lot of batting practice. I had the time of my life being around big-league players again, some of whom I had played with. Then I caught a break. The club needed a new first-base coach. At 31, I was back in the big leagues.

I picked up quite a few things in the two years I coached under Gene Mauch at Montreal. Mauch is an extraordinarily dedicated, hardworking, intelligent baseball man. I threw a lot of batting practice, and I watched and listened. A couple years later there was a change in the Montreal organization, and I was sent to their Denver farm team as a coach. That's where I began working with some good hitters, guys like Andre Dawson, Gary Roenicke, and Warren Cromartie.

Then the Expos sent me to Alberta to manage in the rookie league. Alberta was far from the majors, but I got another break. I had stayed friendly with Don Zimmer ever since I played for him in Salt Lake City in 1970. We were two-of-a-kind, aggressive and hard-working, so we had a lot of respect for each other. In the summer of 1976 Don was living in my house in Andover, Massachusetts, when the Red Sox asked him to take over as manager. Don called me and offered me a job. After twelve years with Boston, I quit and took a job with Chicago. The White Sox are where Charlie Lau coached last, and they have a special devotion to his ideas.

Still, it was with the Red Sox that I developed into a professional hitting coach.

What a thrill to work with the team of my childhood. Suddenly I was no longer working with rookies in Alberta, but with guys like Carl Yastrzemski, Carlton Fisk, and Fred Lynn. I made myself available to them—or any hitter—who wanted extra work.

I'll tell you about one guy, hardly the most famous player, who really impressed me—Jerry Remy, the Red Sox second baseman. Jerry worked hard every day, kept on an even emotional keel, and got the most out of himself. He made himself into a solid .275 lifetime hitter, and it would have been higher if knee injuries hadn't cut short his career. I loved working with Jerry. He believed in what I told him, tried it, and became a much better hitter. That's every bit as satisfying as working with the superstars.

Yaz was another player who set a tremendous example. He absolutely got the most out of himself by exercising tremendous discipline. He'd practice and practice until he could transfer that desire and concentration to the game itself. He kept at it until he was 44 years old. He truly understood what batting practice was all about. It's not about getting loose. It is just what the words say: batting *practice*. At batting practice you want to create the good habits that you take into the game.

These are some other Red Sox hitters I've worked with over the years.

Carl Yastrzemski was not only an excellent hitter—he was also one of the hardest workers in the game.

I'm a strong believer in—maybe even a fanatic about—practice. That's where players improve themselves. There are a lot of theories and philosophies about pitching, fielding, and hitting, but unless you can take them onto the field and make them work, they're useless. The only way to make them work is to perfect them in practice. You take two ballplayers with equal talent, and the one who puts in a lot more time and work will turn out to be the better player. A lot of people might think that he just had more talent in the first place, but the truth is he developed his talent to the point where he became better than the other guy.

There's no better example of "practice makes perfect" in the history of baseball than Pete Rose. He exemplifies what hard work and dedication can do for you. If anyone had speculated 25 years ago, when Pete first came up with Cincinnati, that this rookie second baseman was going to break Ty Cobb's record for hits, he would have been locked up. Today Rose has more hits than any player in history. His records speak for themselves, but the greatest tribute I can give Pete is to say that he squeezed every inch of talent possible out of himself. Pete was totally consumed with hitting. I remember back in 1974 when I was coaching with Montreal, I wandered over to Riverfront Stadium in Cincinnati on an off day. The only player there from either team was Rose, already a 12-year veteran and three-time batting champion. There he was all alone in the batting cage taking batting practice off a pitching machine.

Dwight Evans

Wade Boggs

Carlton Fisk

Don Baylor

Mike Greenwell

Bill Buckner

Marty Barrett

Rich Gedman

Spike Owen

Carney Lansford

Jerry Remy

Ellis Burks

Coaching works the same way. Talent, insight, and theories aren't enough. You could use a degree in psychology as well, because you have to understand people. Sometimes you've got to be understanding, and sometimes you've got to be a drill sergeant. Recognizing when it's time for each approach is not easy. You don't want to give a guy a kick in the pants when what he really needs is a pat on the back. I learned that if Jerry Remy went hitless, that was not the time to talk to him. But you can go talk to Rich Gedman right after a really bad night, and he can use what you tell him.

That Red Sox team I joined in 1977 was one of the finest hitting teams in recent years. The entire team averaged .282; four guys knocked in more than 100 runs and five guys hit 26 or more home runs on the way to a team total of 213. I can't take credit for all the Red Sox hitting successes in my tenure as bullpen coach, and later as hitting and first-base coach. But I'm proud to have contributed whatever I could to the ballclub. What a privilege it was to work with Yaz and see him continue to make a steady contribution to the Red Sox into his 40s. And it has been truly special working with Dwight Evans and watching him improve with age. What an incredible year he had at age 35, when ballplayers are supposed to be slowing down. You seldom hear him mentioned as one of the big stars of the game, but he should be. He's one of the leading home-run hitters of the past decade.

Then there's Bill Buckner, who came to the Red Sox with more than 2,000 career hits but is so dedicated that he was willing to make changes. I hope baseball fans can forget that World Series error he made and see Buckner for the great hitter and dedicated professional he is. At 35, with some gimpy wheels, Bill hit .299, drove in 110 runs, and stole 18 bases to boot.

George Steinbrenner traded Don Baylor from the Yankees, saying Don couldn't hit right-handers anymore. Don worked with me in Boston and had himself a pretty fine year in 1986—against both lefties and righties—with 31 home runs and 94 RBIs.

One thing I have always emphasized to hitters is making contact in order to cut down on strikeouts. The 1986 Red Sox team struck out only 707 times, an incredible 141 times less than any other team in the league. To show it was no fluke, they had the fewest strikeouts in the league again in 1987 and in 1988. In 1988 they again led the majors in runs scored, walks, and batting.

I'll finish with the most incredible hitter I've ever worked with. I'd like to take credit for Wade Boggs, but Wade would be a great hitter even if he had never met me. Still, I don't think I ever had a prouder moment than after the 1985 season, when Wade, after winning the batting crown with a .368 average, was named the team's Most Valuable Player. Accepting the award, Wade pointed to me in the audience and said, "The man who should receive this is over there."

There's no right bat or wrong bat. There is, however, a right or wrong bat for a particular hitter. The right bat is the one the hitter can handle, the one he feels most comfortable with. It's that simple.

At one time, almost all hitters used big bats. They were long and heavy. The theory was: the bigger the bat, the more wood on the ball, the farther the ball went. Babe Ruth supposedly used a bat that was 35 inches long and weighed 40 ounces. That's two and a half pounds, a hefty piece of wood to swing with any efficiency. The modern era's greatest home-run hitter, Hank Aaron, used a bat that was almost as long as the Babe's, but it weighed 32 or 33 ounces.

The trend today—and over the last decade—is toward shorter, lighter bats. Power hitters feel this helps them generate more bat speed and hit the ball out of the park more easily. Contact hitters have gone to the lighter bats as well, for more bat control. You seldom see a bat today over 34 ounces; most major-league hitters use bats weighing between 31 and 34 ounces. Some big, strong guys like Don Baylor or Jim Rice used heavier bats earlier in their careers, but now use lighter ones. Ted Williams used heavy bats early in the season and switched to lighter ones later in the year when he was more tired.

Weight isn't the only decision a hitter has to make about his bat. He has to decide on the thickness of the handle and the barrel of the bat. Many hitters used to use thick-handled bats—we called them bottle bats. Jackie Robinson and Nellie Fox, a couple of Hall of Famers who died tragically young, used them with tremendous success. Another bottle-batter was Manny Sanguillen, the former free-swinging Pirate catcher who had several fine seasons. But I don't think I've seen a bottle bat in the majors since Manny retired almost a decade ago.

However, a lot of guys—probably a majority—still use big-barreled bats. The bigger the barrel of the bat, the more surface there is to hit the ball. I think big-barreled bats are preferable. But when I was a hitter, I didn't use one. I never felt comfortable with the big barrel. The bat felt top-heavy to me. The balance just wasn't right. I liked to use a bat that was more balanced, with the barrel not way out of proportion to the handle. Ultimately, it doesn't matter what kind of bat I tell you is best in theory for hitting. The one that really *is* best is the one with which you feel most comfortable.

Baseball takes tremendous physical skills, but so much of the game is mental. Bats are a good example. Often players can't tell you why they like a certain bat. It just feels good. If the one that feels good weighs 32 ounces and you hand them an identical bat that happens to weigh 31 ounces, they can tell the difference. Some hitters switch bats. They use a 32-ouncer one day and

Thick-handled bats are rarely used these days, but Hall of Famer Nellie Fox hit successfully with one.

a 33-ouncer the next. Hitters can get really psyched over a particular bat—and I don't mean one model—if they get a good streak going. Dwight Evans went on a tear and used the same bat for six weeks. When he broke it one day in Chicago on a base hit, he looked over at me in the coach's box and said, "Walter, I got my money's worth out of that bat." So much of selecting can't be explained. The bat either feels good or it doesn't.

Major-league hitters have no choice when it comes to picking between an aluminum bat and a wooden bat. But all other players right up through college baseball do. Tradition aside, there's no real choice between them. You have to go with aluminum. Aluminum bats are simply more effective. The ball just flies off them, giving hitters a tremendous advantage. That's why college batting averages and power statistics are so inflated. I don't think we'll ever see aluminum bats in the majors. The record books would be filled with asterisks as guys began hitting 70 or more home runs a year.

Batting Gloves

When I first started playing ball, nobody used batting gloves. By the mid-1960s, you began to see them occasionally. Now very few players don't use them. George Brett is the most notable nonbeliever; I guess he just likes the feel of that wood. But he makes up for it by using a lot of pine tar to get a good grip. (In 1983, that resulted in one of the game's bigger controversies when George had a home run temporarily disallowed because he had too much pine tar on his bat.)

Some players wear two gloves, others wear one. It's like golfers—they all wear gloves when they're on the tee, but some take their gloves off when they're standing over a putt. They believe they get a better feel that way. Holding a bat is the same way. Whatever feels the most comfortable, whatever gives you the best grip, that's what you should use.

Unlike many other aspects of hitting, there's not that much to say about the grip. The number-one thing to remember is not to seize the bat with a death grip. A white-knuckle choke hold prevents you from being relaxed at the plate. I advocate a looser grip of the bat. That doesn't mean you should be able to slide a bat through your hands like a pool cue. You can see what I'm talking about best with golfers. They often seem to be milking the golf club as they get ready in their stance; their hands and arms move a lot. They do this to get rid of tension in the hands.

Willie Mays was a terrific example. He used to milk the bat up and down with his fingers. He had so much movement his fingers often came off the bat, but right at the end his grip would settle in and WHAM! Rod Carew also had a very relaxed grip, and he used it to chalk up seven batting crowns, including four in a row from 1972 to 1975. The only other hitters who've ever managed that are Ty Cobb, who won nine in a row from 1907 to 1915, Rogers Hornsby, who won six in a row from 1920 to 1925, and Honus Wagner, who won four in a row from 1906 to 1909. Wade Boggs will join that list if he wins his fourth in a row in 1988.

Ty Cobb and Rod Carew each gripped the bat in a relaxed manner. They didn't tighten up.

You want a relaxed grip because relaxation is one of the keys to hitting. You want to be able to relax all through your swing. When taking a swing, we all have a tendency to tighten up. If you start tight with the bat in a choke

hold, that tension, that tightness, will inevitably spread through your whole body, and you don't want to be tense while hitting.

Obviously, each hitter has to grip the bat where it feels most comfortable in his hand. I simply advise avoiding any extreme grip. Don't hold the bat in your fingers, or in the back of your hand. The swing I teach works best if you hold the bat somewhere in the middle of your hand and somewhere in the middle of your fingers, around the second joint. But again, the key is not where you grab the bat, but the looseness and fluidity with which you grab it. NO DEATH GRIPS!

I advocate keeping your hands together on the bat. Sure, you have a bit more control with your hands spread apart. But there are other ways to achieve bat control, such as choking up. Also, if you split your hands, you lose the snap of the bat and wind up hitting too much with your wrists. It also becomes very difficult to release the swing; you end up with more of a half swing, as though you're chopping at the ball. You can't swing through the ball and get a good follow-through with your hands spread. True, the great Ty Cobb, the man with the highest career batting average of anyone who has ever played the game, held the bat with his hands split. But Cobb was one of a kind. You shouldn't imitate him.

Even sluggers such as Ted Williams choked up on the bat in some situations.

Every young batter hears a great deal about choking up. From his very first days in Little League, he's told—at the very least—to choke up with two strikes in order to have more bat control. I can't disagree with that. If a hitter feels the need for more bat control, choking up is a good way to accomplish it. What I take issue with is telling hitters they *have* to choke up. Each hitter has to decide what feels comfortable to him.

The Red Sox have been blessed over the last 50 years with three truly great left-fielders, and each handled this matter a little differently. Ted Williams, who was the greatest hitter of them all, inched up on his bat just a little in his later years, and it helped him hit .388 when he was 39 years old. Jim Rice is as big and strong a hitter as there is. Still, in certain situations he'll choke up three or four inches. He's had a lot of success doing that. But Carl Yastrzemski just couldn't choke up, even at 43 years old. It didn't feel comfortable to him. So he found another answer—he went to a shorter, lighter bat. This gave him more bat control, and is a perfectly viable option.

The Grip: Summary

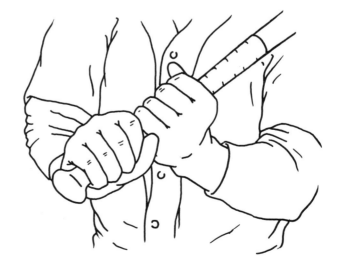

1 **Keep a loose, relaxed grip before you swing. Don't strangle the bat.**
2 **Grip the bat in the middle of your hands and fingers.**
3 **Keep your hands together on the bat— don't split them.**
4 **Choke up for better bat control—but only if it feels comfortable.**
5 **Using a shorter, lighter bat is another way to improve bat control.**

This is the stance I prefer most. My feet are
parallel, neither closed nor open, and my
knees are bent slightly. I am waiting for the
pitch with my weight back, not straight up—on
the balls of my feet, not on my heels. My hands
are positioned so that my bat is at a 45-degree
angle to the ground, and my head stands out
from my shoulder so that I have a clear view of
the pitcher with both eyes.

The stance is the foundation for everything that follows. In some ways, it is the most important component of how to hit. If the stance isn't strong, what comes after can't be strong. Without a well-structured stance, both the stride and the swing will be less efficient, less powerful than they could be. Without a balanced stance, the whole swing crumbles. The key word is *balance*.

I mentioned that perhaps the greatest hitter in baseball history, Ty Cobb, had an unorthodox grip, one I can't recommend. Similarly, some great hitters as well as some very good hitters have had and currently have what I consider unbalanced stances. Stan Musial, the greatest St. Louis Cardinal ever, had an extraordinary stance, one that looked unbalanced. Still, he managed to set a lot of National League hitting records and cruise into the Hall of Fame. Rod Carew used many different stances, one for every conceivable occasion. A lot of them were unbalanced—some open, some closed—but he had the talent to make them work. Some pretty good hitters, like the California Angels' Brian Downing or Red Sox catcher Rich Gedman, have unorthodox stances that are exceptionally open. Each has managed to hit well in spite of it.

Rich Gedman knows I don't like his stance. It's a very open stance; he developed it because he was having trouble with inside pitches. But the open stance has plenty of drawbacks. The hips tend to open prematurely, the batter can lose sight of the baseball, and as a result he may "fall off" the ball. When Rich first showed up with his stance after winter ball in Venezuela, I told him, "I don't particularly like it. I won't say it's not going to work, but I don't like it. To make it work, you're going to have to be incredibly disciplined." And he has been. A couple of All-Star appearances testify to that. But for most hitters, there's just no point in putting themselves to that test. A square stance is by far the most efficient. Any other stance forces you to waste energy by moving to get into the proper position to hit the ball. Any time you have excess movement, you have more opportunities for the swing to break down, for things to go wrong.

For most hitters, I recommend a balanced, workable stance. To achieve that without bothering to read the rest of the chapter, spend about a year at Fenway Park in Boston watching Wade Boggs. His stance is nearly perfect—and it's the same every time he steps up to the plate. Wade understands that good hitting is predictable, mappable, chartable. It begins in the feet, travels up through the legs, through the hips, to the shoulders, to the arms, until it finally works its way up to the head. A balanced stance helps assure that the swing will progress that way properly. This concept does not apply only to baseball. Every sport, every athletic skill, requires great balance.

Feet

Balance, as I've said, starts with the feet. Your feet shouldn't be too close together, nor too far apart. Place them somewhere about shoulder width, with the front and rear feet parallel to each other; in other words, neither should be closer to the plate than the other.

Next, get into a square stance—a position essentially parallel to the plate. When you stride straight ahead at the pitcher, you want to be able to extend your arms and cover the entire plate. You don't want to have to step toward or away from the plate to handle the strike zone. Ideally, when you extend the bat, it should reach over the far end of the plate. The meat of the bat should cover the outside half of the plate.

This square stance eliminates extraneous movement and makes your swing more efficient. There's less shoulder movement, less head movement, less eye movement. With either a closed or open stance, there are some pitches in the strike zone that you have to move away from or stride toward to be able to hit. But if you are square to the plate, you don't have to contort your body—twisting, turning, or diving—to handle any pitch in the strike zone. With a closed stance, too often you're forced to come off the ball and hit on your heels. With an open stance, you're lunging in, almost stumbling toward the ball.

It's really just common sense. If your feet are square, you'll achieve better balance than if your feet are crooked, regardless of whether they are closed crooked or open crooked.

Head

As a hitter, I had a closed stance. At the time I thought a closed stance was preferable because it would keep me on the ball. It kept me from flying open. It kept my head on the ball. But I overlooked some things—most notably the baseball. The closed stance blocked off my vision. I couldn't see the pitcher and, even more important, the baseball, with my back eye. If I had closed my front eye, I would have been blind at the plate. With a square stance, your head is in the correct position, allowing you to see the ball clearly with both eyes, not blocking vision in one eye.

It's important for the head to be as square as the stance. I ask kids, "Would you read a sign with your head tilted or upright?" The answer is obvious. You want to see the ball with both eyes, both of them undistorted. You can't do that when your head is sideways, only when it is erect.

Beginners are not the only ones who need to learn this lesson. A lot of major leaguers get into the bad habit of tucking their head behind the front shoulder. Then they tell me, "I'm not picking the ball up. I'm not seeing it well." When I check out their stance, the first thing I look at is the head. Ninety-nine percent of the time they're tucking the head back behind the shoulder. To prove my point, I stand on the mound and tell them to close their front eye. They can't see me on the mound. I ask them how they'd fare if a ball was coming in on them at 90 miles per hour.

Weight

The next key is weight distribution. As in virtually every other sport, you want your weight on the balls of your feet, not on your heels. Whenever an athlete is getting ready to perform an act—returning a tennis ball, or defending against a drive in basketball—he gets ready by putting his weight on the balls of his feet. If you lie back on your heels, you won't be able to move quickly at all. You'll lack balance. A lot of hitters understand that they should put their weight on the balls of their feet, but they don't actually do it.

Most players try to achieve proper weight balance by bending at the knees. But the best way is to bend at the waist first, making sure you distribute your weight on the balls of your feet—and only then, bend at the knees. You'll feel the difference immediately. All of a sudden you feel the weight focused on the balls of your feet, and you're aware that you have better balance. This is a routine that every hitter should practice again and again. It should be a constant, an absolute. In fact, all hitting should be a series of constant rituals that enable the hitter to attain the same correct stance every time. Too many hitters, when they get into a slump, start changing their stance, trying this and that. But that usually makes the slump worse, and the player more frustrated. Instead, you should practice day-in, day-out with game intensity until you can assume the correct stance every time, until you can achieve it with blinders on—undistracted. Get the correct technique, and the hits will come.

Hands

At the end of the stride every good hitter has his hands in the same position and the bat at the same angle. The hands wind up at shoulder height, a few inches off the rear shoulder, and the bat at a 45-degree angle. It doesn't matter whether the hitter started with his hands low or high; they wind up in the same place.

Just remember that in a split second you're going to have to get your hands and the bat to this shoulder-high position with the bat at a 45-degree angle. If you have trouble getting there, start your stance with your hands and bat closer to that position. You have to have your hands in a comfortable position. But start as close to that desired final position as possible because the more your hands and bat move, the more room there is for error. More on this in the next chapter.

Wade Boggs

Rich Gedman

Dwight Evans

George Brett

Here are four stances that are all a little different but that share several characteristics. Wade Boggs's stance is perfectly balanced. He is already back a little bit, but when the pitch is released, he will move even further back. Rich Gedman's stance is unorthodox because it is so open, but it is still basically sound. It works because his weight is on his back side, and his head is in the right spot. Like Gedman, Dwight Evans positions himself farther back in his stance than does Boggs. Although it looks a little unusual, his stance is very effective. By picking up his front heel, he can place more weight on his back foot. His feet are square and positioned shoulder-width apart. Notice also that his knees are bent slightly to ensure that his weight is on the balls of his feet. George Brett also lays back in his stance, but he is balanced and ready to hit with his bat at a 45-degree angle; his head is set so that he can see the pitch clearly with both eyes.

1-2   **3**   **4-7**

The Stance: Summary

1 Start with a balanced stance, square to the plate.
2 Plant your feet about shoulder width, with both feet parallel to each other.

3 Be sure that the bat can be extended slightly beyond the plate, so that the meat of the bat covers the outside half of the plate.

4 Keep your head erect, so you can see the mound with both eyes.
5 Put your weight on the balls of your feet.
6 Bend first at the waist, then at the knees, to assure proper weight distribution.
7 Keep your hands as close as possible to the position they will wind up in at the end of the stride.
8 Create a routine that enables you to take the same stance every time you prepare to hit.

The weight shift involves getting back before moving forward to start the stride. Because I prefer to start back in my stance, the move back is actually a part of the stance. Some players start their stances straight up and then make a clear and definite move back. Either way, these are the things to remember about the weight shift: Transfer your weight to your back side and position your hands so that the bat moves toward the launch position—at a 45-degree angle to the ground. Keep your head erect so that both of your eyes can see the pitcher clearly, and keep your knees bent so that your weight stays on the balls of your feet. Once you get back to this position, you're ready to begin your stride forward.

It's commonly assumed that, once you're in your stance, you move directly into a stride. But before you take that stride, there is one other component of hitting that is essential to taking a good swing at the ball. Again, this component holds true in every sport. Think of throwing a baseball, swinging a golf club, throwing a punch, shooting a hockey puck. Athletes engaged in these activities are trying to propel an object forward—just like the batter. What do they all have in common? In every one of these activities, they move *back* before they move *forward.*

We don't even have to talk about sports to make this point. Say you're really angry, and you want to let the world know it by slamming a door. You wouldn't just put your hand on the door and push. You would take the door, draw it back, and then slam it. Your first motion is backward to create additional power. Anytime you want to propel an object forward, in our case a baseball with a bat, first you must shift your weight backward.

Of course, hitters have been moving back before going forward since the game was invented. With a lot of hitters, it's a very exaggerated movement. They begin back in their stance, resulting in what appears to be an unbalanced stance. Dwight Evans is one example; Cecil Cooper was another. Rod Carew sat back in his stance. With a hitter like Wade Boggs, who stands square with his weight apparently distributed evenly, the move back is not nearly as obvious. But it's there. Wade Boggs shifts back (Ted Williams did it the same way) by cocking his front leg inward. This creates a move back, a definite weight shift. If you begin in that even stance and turn your front knee in, you wind up planting your weight on top of your rear foot—thus creating the weight shift.

Some hitters have gone to incredible extremes to get that weight back. People laughed at Mel Ott's hitting style; he actually lifted his front leg up before he hit. But nobody laughed after he hit more than 500 homers and entered the Hall of Fame. Ott was doing the same thing Boggs does— shifting his weight to his rear foot before he went forward. He just did it more obviously than most.

I certainly don't want to recommend Ott's style because, although it succeeded in achieving the correct weight distribution, it wasn't as balanced as I'd like. Ott was an exceptional hitter and could handle it, but most hitters can't. Once again, balance is essential.

In fact, balance is another reason you go back before forward. If you look at pictures of good hitters at the conclusion of their stride, their weight is neither back nor forward. They land with their weight distributed about evenly. If you don't go back in your stance in the first place, when you stride forward you'll wind up too far forward, unbalanced. Your head will

Wade Boggs

Rich Gedman

wind up somewhere out over your front foot. Your only other choice would be to take a short stride and hit practically flat-footed.

I recommend starting the stance balanced, moving back to an unbalanced position, and then striding forward to regain that balance. You could start balanced, take a very short stride, and stay balanced. But you'd be hitting without any power, without the surge that rocking back and propelling yourself forward provides. I suggest starting back about the time the pitcher's arm goes back. That provides some easy-to-remember symmetry: Start back when the pitcher does.

A strange thing happens during this weight shift. I tell my hitters to lead with the lower half of the body. As the pitcher's arm goes back, the hitter turns his front leg and starts the lower half of his body back. Obviously, the top half will follow. But as the top half moves back, the bottom half will have already been back and essentially have started forward into the stride. It's as if the hitter's body—if only for a millisecond—is moving in two different directions.

Hank Aaron had as good a weight shift as any hitter I ever watched. He needed it. He was strong, but he weighed only about 180 pounds. He needed great technique to hit those 755 homers that made him the career home-run leader. Aaron was superb at getting to that balanced position and maximizing his power.

Wade Boggs, Rich Gedman, George Brett, and Dwight Evans all have excellent weight shifts. This photograph of Boggs shows him just as he is getting back; he cocks his front leg to help him make that move. Gedman and Brett are all the way back. Note that their front heels are off the ground, ready to start the stride forward. Brett, in particular, is

George Brett

Dwight Evans

But even Aaron didn't get it perfect all the time. One of the old hitting adages is that you've got to hit off your back foot. If you watch old films of Aaron, you'll see that he hit a lot of home runs when his back foot was actually off the ground at the point of contact. In fact, I don't believe anybody has ever hit a home run with that back foot truly planted in the ground. There are many different degrees of weight shift. In every one of them the heel comes off the ground. Everybody comes off that back foot to some extent. If you can't be evenly balanced, it's better to be forward rather than back.

Obviously, some guys can stay back and still hit home runs. But they are exceptions—the biggest, strongest guys. Jim Rice can do it. He may look totally fooled, have his weight back, and still muscle the ball out of the park. Reggie Jackson also could muscle home runs. But even though Reggie had true OOMPH in his swing—and it thrilled a lot of fans—he lacked a little technique. Charlie Lau worked with Reggie one year to help him settle his swing and find balance, rhythm, and fluidity. That year Reggie slammed 41 home runs and hit .300, the only time in his career he reached the .300 mark.

Let's talk about another great hitter, Don Mattingly. Don is nicely balanced when he first gets into his stance. But as the pitcher goes into his windup, Mattingly starts to move his back foot and sort of sits back on it. It's his way of getting back—his trigger. He starts back earlier than most great

able to generate a tremendous amount of power because his weight shift is extreme. His front foot actually comes off the ground as he shifts completely back. Evans's shift back is similar to Brett's, except he holds his hands a little higher, placing his bat closer to the launch position.

hitters, but the important thing is that he does get back, not when he gets there. Don learned his weight-shift variation from Lou Piniella, who was an outstanding hitter, and Lou learned it from Charlie Lau. Lau taught Piniella the importance of getting back and then leading with the legs; only then have you got something to hit with. When Mattingly came up, he was a .300 hitter in the minor leagues, but he didn't have any juice. He'd reach out and slap the ball to left field. When he learned how to use his legs and get his whole body into his swing, he added a whole new dimension. He can still slap the ball to left field if he wants to, but he can also hit it out of the park 30 or 40 times a year.

There's one final reason that movement in the stance is important. Anybody who plays this game will eventually fail. It may be in Little League, striking out in front of your parents, grandparents, brothers, and sisters, or it can be in the seventh game of the World Series. Even the best hitters aren't going to do much better than get three hits every 10 times they're up at the plate. Seven times in every 10 at-bats, the hitter is going to fail. Failure creates tension. It creates embarassment. It creates a fear of more failure.

When a hitter feels tense, somebody—maybe his hitting coach, maybe his best friend, maybe his wife—will tell him, "You looked tight at the plate. Relax." That's not bad advice but it falls into the "easier said than done" category.

The way to relax is to get movement into your stance. In every sport, movement is a key to relaxing. Watch tennis great Jimmy Connors waiting for a serve. He moves his feet and sways back and forth. Watch any professional golfer as he addresses the ball on the tee. Before he begins his swing, he moves and sways. This helps him to relax.

Another advantage of movement is that it enables athletes to be more explosive. Brooks Robinson, one of the greatest third basemen who ever lived, had tremendous range even though he was a slow runner. When Robinson readied himself in the field, he kept his feet moving. This enabled him to take off as soon as the ball was hit. He reminded me of a car revving its engine before a drag race. Watch the Boston Celtics's Dennis Johnson play defense against speedsters — guys faster than him — such as Isiah Thomas or Magic Johnson. Ever wonder why they can't just blow by him? One reason is that he's always moving his feet. He's creating energy that enables him, when it's time to move decisively, to be quicker and more effective.

Just as it's vital for athletes in all these sports to move, it's also critical for a hitter, because in half a second he has to take a 90-mile-per-hour fastball and make it go the other way. The great hitters in baseball have been characterized by a certain fluidity and grace. Very few great hitters have been still or stiff at the plate. Carl Yastrzemski was an exception, but in his later years even Yaz adapted his stance to add some movement. He began rotating his bat in a circle, and that really helped him relax and stay fluid at the plate. When I was in the minors, coaches used to say, "Get in the batter's box and don't move 'til you hit the baseball." This, I learned years too late, is the worst thing you can do.

So keep moving—nice, easy movement—as long as the pitcher holds onto the ball. Never stop just because the pitcher is taking his time. Smart, experienced pitchers know that the tenser and tighter the hitter is, the more it's to the hurler's advantage. Gaylord Perry was as savvy and tough a pitcher as I've ever seen; he won over 300 games. Sometimes he'd hold onto the ball and let hitters grind themselves into a hole. You could see them getting tighter and tighter each second he stalled. Keep moving, and if the pitcher stalls too long and you find yourself getting tense, step out of the box and start your stance all over again.

Only at the very end, just before you begin your stride, should you quiet down in your stance. At that point, extra movement is a distraction. It's just like a golfer about to drive from the tee. He moves a lot as he readies himself to swing, but just before he takes the club back, he settles down. His stance becomes quiet. It's the same for a hitter the instant before he swings.

Certain players look very relaxed at the plate. Wade Boggs and George Brett have a pace and movement in their stance that helps them to get rid of tension in their hands, arms, and legs. One way to stay relaxed is to move the bat continually just before settling into your stance—the way Boggs and Brett do.

The Weight Shift: Summary

1 Shift your weight back before you stride forward.
2 A good way to shift weight is to cock your front leg (or turn your front knee) inward.
3 Develop a fluid weight shift. First back, then forward, leading with the lower half of your body.
4 Keep movement in your stance as well as in your grip. Don't be a statue at the plate.
5 Quiet down just before you begin your stride.

1-2

3

Once the stance and weight shift are accomplished, it's time to stride forward. You do this by leading with the lower half of your body in an aggressive but controlled manner. By that I mean you should make a definite move forward, but don't lunge. That move forward should be directly at the pitcher, not toward the first or third base line. When you finish the stride, land with your knees bent and your front foot closed so that you'll remain balanced —on the balls of your feet — with the bat at the launch position —a 45-degree angle to the ground. At all times, keep your head positioned so that you are seeing the ball clearly with both eyes.

Constructing a baseball swing is something like building a house. The stance is the foundation, the stride is the first floor, and the swing is the second floor. If you don't build those first two parts right, the whole house will fall down. Too many hitters don't really concentrate on that first floor; they think of the stride as part of the swing. But the stride is a very critical part of hitting. A good stride with proper timing and mechanisms puts you in a strong position to hit the baseball. With a poor stride, you wind up with a weak swing. You can have a perfect stance, but a weak stride will ruin everything. It doesn't mean you'll never hit the ball or get a base hit. It does mean you're not using your body to its best advantage.

There is one major misconception hitters have about the stride. They believe that they don't actually begin their stride until the ball leaves the pitcher's hand. The truth is, every major-league hitter starts his stride before the ball leaves the pitcher's hand. In their minds, hitters may not be starting their stride until the pitch is thrown, but their bodies know better. The forward stride begins while the pitcher's arm is descending—but before the pitch is thrown.

This requires great timing, and great hitters work hard on this aspect of their game. Watch Don Mattingly in the on-deck circle. He doesn't check out the crowd or pose for pictures. He studies the pitcher's delivery so that he knows exactly when to begin his stride. He knows the importance of the stride.

The game's best hitters have a wide variety of strides. But they all begin at the same time—before the ball is released. That rule is absolute. Start the stride before the ball is released. You can't step and hit at the same time; you have to step first and *then* hit.

It's easy enough to prove this point. Just try working out on one of those newer pitching machines where the ball comes flying out of a hole. There's no way to time it. I prefer the old pitching machines—we called them "Iron Mikes." They had arms, and batters could see the arm descend and time the release, just as if it were a real pitcher. With the new machines, the ball just pops out of a hole, and the hitter has to wait until the ball is released to start his stride. As a result, many hitters start their strides too late and get caught standing flat-footed. These new pitching machines make it very difficult to practice, and can mess up a hitter.

Most hitters intuitively start their stride at the right time—even if they're not aware of it. However, many don't stride in the right direction. The correct stride is straight ahead, right at the pitcher. That isn't easy for everyone to do. A lot of young hitters stride away from the pitcher. This is called "stepping in the bucket." Frankly, most hitters do that because they're

Don Baylor has been hit by a pitched ball more often than any other hitter in base- ball history. However, he doesn't get hurt because he strides in a balanced manner and lands on the balls of his feet. This ena- bles him to turn away from the pitch in time.

a little scared of being hit by the ball. That's nothing to be ashamed of; it's human nature. Oddly enough, the hitters who step away from the pitcher to avoid getting hit are putting themselves in a position to be hurt worse when it happens.

Take Don Baylor, who has the dubious distinction of having set the all-time Major League record for being hit by a pitch. He strides straight at the pitcher. And because he strides correctly, he lands correctly—on the balls of his feet. That gives him the proper balance both to hit and to get out of the way of a pitched ball. He can turn or duck his head—always toward the catcher, not the pitcher—and, when he is hit, usually manage to take it on the meaty part of the arm or shoulder. But when you stride away from the pitcher, you wind up with your weight on your heels. You have no balance and little maneuverability. If a pitch is headed at you, about all you can do to get out of the way is fall on your rear end.

The biggest single flaw among young hitters, including some really promising hitters, is their tendency to open up their hips too soon. When you stride away from the baseball, you can't help but open up your hips. Instead, stride straight ahead, so that you land with your front foot closed. By landing in a closed rather than an open position, you remain square to the pitcher. Square shoulders. Square hips. Head down.

To understand this, again there's no hitter better to watch than Wade Boggs. He strides straight ahead and keeps his balance completely.

I'd guess that about 90 percent of all hitters in the major leagues land somewhat open. If it still isn't clear why this is bad, watch some golf tournaments. Golfers stay square to the ball. Often their swing will carry through right over their front foot. This sometimes makes them look as if they've lost their balance, but by being square to the tee they get all their power and control into that swing.

There are no hard-and-fast rules about the correct length of the stride. Great hitters like Stan Musial and George Brett have had relatively long strides, but Joe DiMaggio managed to hit in 56 straight games with a very short stride. Often, smaller guys have longer strides, because they need more of a weight shift to power the ball. Big, strong guys often have short strides, because they use their upper-body muscle to drive the ball out of the park. My major concern with a short stride is that the hitter sometimes loses aggressiveness at the plate.

Some coaches suggest keeping the stride between three and five inches, but I don't believe that's important. It's the direction the stride takes, not its length, that counts. Take the stride that's comfortable for you and make sure it's directed straight at the pitcher.

Whatever its length, the stride must be aggressive. I don't mean hitters should leap at the ball so that they lose their balance, and thus lose control of their swing. Often, hitters who have problems with lunging are advised to "stay back." They may then overcompensate and make the opposite mistake. Staying back can be just as bad as lunging forward.

The question is how to move forward in the correct way. The answer is fairly simple—lead with your legs, in particular with your front leg. Leading with your legs lets you be aggressive while your upper body stays back. That way, you're striding powerfully and staying back at the same time. Of course, your upper body will come forward a bit, but it won't be way out in front.

When your foot lands, it's important that, having taken all that trouble to start on the balls of your feet, you stay there. Keep telling yourself to land with your toe closed—just as you started—because that way you'll stay on the balls of your feet. Open up, and you'll land on your heels and lack balance, control, and power in your swing. You shouldn't go into contortions trying to keep that front foot closed; it's OK if your foot opens up a little. In fact, you may want to do that deliberately sometimes, particularly if you're "cheating" a little and looking for an inside pitch. If you think the

Wade Boggs

Dwight Evans

pitch is moving outside, you might close up a little more. But no hitter wants to be guessing all the time. It's best to stride down the middle and keep all your options open.

All this contradicts a lot of what's been said and written about hitting through the years. Some coaches still insist that you can't hit if you land with your front toe closed. I say the opposite; you can't hit as effectively if you land with your foot too open. One reason coaches don't believe this is that it's hard to picture that landing.

To see the difference, imagine you're stepping on an egg instead of stepping on a bug. When you step on a bug, you stomp it. This is aggressiveness without control. I want a hitter to make an aggressive move, but not a wild one. The landing—on that egg—should be firm but controlled. A perfect example is Wade Boggs; he has an agressive stride with a soft landing, and that's the combination you want.

Many misconceptions about hitting have developed through the years. That's why the use of cameras and videotape has revolutionized hitting. For the first time, hitters can really see what they're doing, and break down each at-bat into all its parts. I used to argue with Don Baylor about how hitters landed. Don's a great hitter and a knowledgeable baseball man, but he couldn't believe that when a hitter completes his stride, he lands with the

Rich Gedman

Here are three different hitters as they complete their stride. They all look remarkably similar—bat in the launch position, head looking over the shoulders directly at the pitched ball, hips closed. Each is square to the target and balanced, neither too far forward nor too far back, with their legs positioned directly below their upper body. Note also that each hitter has his front foot closed. Boggs's and Evans's stride look almost identical, while Gedman's stride is noticeably longer.

front leg bent. He was certain that he landed stiff-legged. So I took Don up to the video room to watch himself at bat. I had the operator stop the action the instant Don's foot hit the ground. When he stopped it, I asked, "Donald, is your leg bent?" He said, "Yeah." Then we moved ahead a couple of frames and I said, "See, it's stiff now." All he could say was, "I'll be damned." It's hard to imagine while you're hitting—it all happens too fast.

There are so many things the camera has helped us see clearly for the first time. For example, if you shoot videotape of good hitters and slow the footage down, you'll see that when their stride is completed—no matter how differently they stood or held the bat—their hands and the bat wind up in virtually identical positions. This goes for every good hitter, from Wade Boggs through Hank Aaron back to Babe Ruth and Ty Cobb. Their bat is extended at a 45-degree angle, about shoulder height and a couple of inches slightly behind the tip of the shoulder. We'll discuss this further. The good hitters get there so fast that you can't see it until you slow it down on film, but they all get there. If you can get there with proper technique and balance, you're ready to take your swing.

The Stride: Summary

1 Start your stride before the pitcher releases the ball.
2 Take whatever length stride is comfortable for you, but aim it right at the pitcher.
3 Make an aggressive stride, but don't lunge or leap.
4 Lead with your legs, not your upper body.
5 You started your stride closed. You want to finish it closed.
6 Don't end your stride by stomping. "Step on an egg."
7 When you land, the bat should be positioned shoulder-high and slightly behind the shoulder, extended at a 45-degree angle.

1-4

5-7

Swinging a baseball bat should be an easy thing to learn. Any hitter with talent can have a technically sound swing—compact and level. However, most hitters have too many misconceptions compounded by years of faulty batting techniques. So it's not just a matter of teaching them how to swing, but helping them unlearn what they're already doing. This isn't just classroom philosophy; I know because I spent my career hitting the wrong way.

As a player, I hit left-handed. It was drummed into me that the top hand—in my case, the left hand—was the key. So I worked to make my left hand strong and repeated to myself again and again, "Top hand over." I can't change my hitting stats now, but I know that I could have been a better hitter if only I had forgotten about that top hand.

The top hand mainly provides support. It adds stability, and cushions the impact when the bat hits the ball. That's why all the best hitters know to keep that top hand underneath at the point of contact, not over as I was taught. When the bat hits the ball, the top hand should be underneath the bat. This may contradict what seems logical and natural to a lot of hitters. Most righties bat right-handed, so they expect their right hand, which is the top hand when they hold the bat, to be the dominant one. But this just isn't the case. The bottom hand is the power hand and the top hand is just along for the ride.

Here's an easy way to prove that having the top hand over the bat leads to a weak hitting position. Stand at the plate and have someone toss you a basketball. When you hit the basketball with your top hand over, the bat practically flies out of your hands. That's because the top hand isn't in a position to provide any support. When that top hand is turned underneath in the correct position, you can hit the basketball and absorb the shock. The bat is stable and stays in your hands. Hitters who have trouble keeping the top hand from coming over wind up beating the ball into the ground a great deal of the time.

The next goal is to move the bat into position to hit the baseball. To start, make a descending blow away from your body with the bottom hand, as if you were aiming to hit something with the back of your hand. The move resembles a karate chop. Many hitters do exactly the opposite. Rather than starting the bottom hand down at an angle, they start by lifting their hand at an upward angle. The effect of this is obvious. If point A is where they are holding the bat and point B is where they hit the ball, by starting the swing upward they're creating a loop in their swing—the equivalent of a long, scenic route from point A to point B.

The shortest swing is the most efficient way to hit the ball. The loop not only deprives the batter of power, but it reduces his accuracy. That's why

I start my swing by leading with my bottom
hand and bringing the bat on a downward
plane to the ball. This is the most direct path
and thus the quickest and most efficient way
to put the bat on the ball. At the same time,
my back heel comes off the ground and my
hips open up. My eyes are focused directly
on the ball.

This is the moment of truth—when the ball meets the bat. Note that I'm still leading with my bottom hand. My top hand remains underneath; it doesn't roll over. My weight shift is complete; my front leg is still stiff. My back leg, with my heel pointing up in the air, looks like the letter L. My bottom hand is extended and my front toe is closed. Most importantly, at all times my head remains down, directed toward the ball. This is the key moment in the swing, not only because it's when the ball gets hit, but because it's the point at which the motion of the swing is no longer down, but starts its ascent upward.

hitters who have a loopy swing, those with pronounced uppercuts, are breaking-ball hitters; they don't have to move the bat as quickly to hit a curve. But these guys have problems with the fastball. A good pitcher just keeps feeding them fastballs—fastballs up, fastballs in—until it looks as if the batter has a hole in his swing. The shorter and faster the swing, the longer a hitter can wait to commit himself. He can lay off the fastball, which helps when it turns out to be a ball in the dirt.

People insist that you can't teach bat speed; either you have it or you don't. I say you *can* teach bat speed with a simple lesson: Longer is slower, shorter is quicker. Shorten a guy's swing, and you can increase the speed of his bat. By starting down with that bottom hand, you get the barrel of the bat out front—and that's a quick stroke.

What confuses a lot of people is the argument that you can't hit a baseball swinging down. But I'm not talking about swinging down. I'm talking about *starting* down. You start down to get your bat in position for the swing. As you start your swing to the ball, the bat should be level (although it's OK if it naturally goes up very slightly). The main point is not to hit the ball during the downward motion. You want to hit the ball out in front of you. At that point, your swing is level or going slightly up.

Such great hitters as Dwight Evans and Jim Rice have a lot in common. They both lead with their bottom hand, keeping their top hand underneath. Their front leg is stiff and their back leg forms an L.

Wade Boggs has tremendous discipline of the head. His head is on the ball for every pitch all of the time—even if the pitch ends up in the catcher's mitt.

What do Dave Winfield, Jim Rice, Carl Yastrzemski, and Wade Boggs have in common? Each keeps his head down on the ball.

Once you are standing right, striding right, and swinging right, we get to the real key to hitting. Keep your head down—just as with golf, tennis, or almost any other sport. Where your head goes, your body follows. Little League coaches have been trying to teach this to their kids for years, but most go about it slightly wrong. They tell their hitters, "Keep your eye on the ball." But they don't say how to do it.

I tell my hitters to put their heads down so they can see the ball more clearly. That's *how* to keep your eye on the ball—by keeping your head down. It's really no different from learning how to field a ground ball. Coaches have always taught kids correctly to keep their head down when fielding. When a fielder keeps his head down, his glove stays down and he literally follows the ball into his glove.

But although coaches have always taught "watch the ball into the glove," they have rarely taught "watch the ball onto the bat." Hitting works the same way as fielding, so it's essential to develop what I call a discipline of the head. Many hitters learned this as keeping their shoulder down, but the head drives the shoulder. If the head is down, the shoulder will be down too. Keep your head down and follow the ball all the way in. Even if you're not swinging at the pitch, you should still follow the ball all the way into the catcher's glove.

Dave Winfield

Jim Rice

Carl Yastrzemski

Wade Boggs

This is a great habit to get into, and some of the best hitters in baseball have made a practice of it. Pete Rose always did it. Wade Boggs always does it. To watch the ball into the catcher's mitt, you have to keep your head down. If you don't keep your head down all the way, you don't really see the baseball travel the last two or three feet. Many hitters hit that way during their entire careers, and they think they see the baseball perfectly well. But that last couple of feet they're really seeing—and swinging at—a blur.

The position of the head affects not only the sight of the ball, but the swing as well. If your head goes up too early, the whole rhythm of the swing gets out of whack. Your shoulders and hips will be positioned incorrectly, and it's almost impossible to begin the swing from the correct spot. So keeping the head down is truly critical—perhaps the most essential component of the entire swing.

With all that said, I really don't expect most hitters to be able to keep their head down as long as Wade Boggs does. Just be sure that your head is down at the point of contact. Still, by being obsessive about the head and exaggerating how long you keep it down, you increase the likelihood that it will actually be down through the point of contact.

Keeping the head down is not an easy habit to develop. Hitters have a lot of ego, and they love to see where the ball goes. Or to put it more kindly, they are anxious to see where the ball is headed. But you don't need to see where the ball goes to start running hard toward first base. I remember Charlie Lau trying to drum this lesson into young hitters. He was pitching batting practice at Yankee Stadium, and one of New York's promising young hitters deposited a couple of balls in the upper deck. Each time, his face would light up and his eyes would follow the ball all the way into the seats. Finally, Charlie got fed up and yelled at him, "Hey, don't watch the ball after you hit it. Let *me* watch it."

If you make contact and then watch the ball, you can still hit adequately. But if you get in the habit of picking up your head after you hit the ball, occasionally you will lift your head too early. All it takes is lifting your head a split second too soon and you're lost. It's a good way to start a long slump.

To be safe, don't let your head pop up at all. That's what I mean by "discipline of the head." I try to give the hitter as much room for error as possible. Sure, he might wind up keeping his head down too long. But a split second too long is much better than a split second too soon. Some hitters get confused and say, "I understand keeping my head down with a low pitch, but how can I do it with a high pitch?" The answer is that your head isn't down as much with a high pitch as a low one—but it's still down. In fact, if the ball is thrown high and you put your head too far down, you may actually lose sight of the ball. Your eyes will be below it.

The lower the pitch, the lower the head. There's no single level that your head should be on for every pitch. I'm not just talking about high and low pitches, but inside and outside pitches as well. On an outside pitch, move your head down toward the middle of the plate. On an inside pitch, move your head down toward the point at which you're making contact. Don't put your head down to the same spot every time. There are different spots for different points of contact with the ball.

Follow-Through

Many hitters think that once they've made contact with the ball, the swing is essentially over. But what you do after you hit the ball directly affects what happens to the ball you hit. Practically every other athletic skill— swinging a golf club or tennis racquet, shooting a free throw, passing a football, and certainly pitching a baseball—places a lot of emphasis on the follow-through. But you almost never hear about it in swinging a bat.

Most hitters can create a better follow-through by releasing their top hand from the bat at a certain point in the follow-through. Many have criticized this notion. However, hitters have been taking their hand off the bat since the game was invented. Old movies of Hall-of-Famers Willie Mays and Ernie Banks show they released their top hand on every swing. There are even pictures showing Babe Ruth taking his hand off the bat.

Not every hitter should release the bat. Some can get the bat to the ball, drive the bat up and through the ball, and have terrific extension and follow-through while keeping both hands on the bat. Hank Aaron had a really high finish with both hands on the bat, and nobody is going to quarrel with the way he hit the baseball. Don Baylor and Gary Carter are a couple of power hitters who have a high finish without releasing the bat. But many hitters can't do that because their top hand is too dominant. It rolls over too soon and when that happens, you can't achieve a proper follow-through with a nice high finish.

If you compare the motion of your swing to the motion of a clock, the top hand shouldn't roll over until about three o'clock if you hit right-handed and nine o'clock if you hit left-handed. That's well into the follow-through. If at that point the top hand threatens to overpower your swing and cut short the follow-through, simply remove it from the bat (a little earlier when the ball is outside, a little later when it's inside). This simple, workable technique will ensure an efficient follow-through. Take Fred Lynn. Sometimes he holds onto the bat, and other times he lets go. In my mind, when his hand comes off, his swing is better—more fluid, more efficient, and more powerful.

Both hands remain on the bat well after the ball is hit. As the swing moves in an upward path, my top hand, which has been underneath until this point, begins to roll over my bottom hand. This allows me to move my bat up in a fluid manner and finish with a high follow-through. The point at which the top hand rolls over is critical—the correct time is when my bat is approximately at nine o'clock in the circle of my swing (three o'clock for right-handed hitters). If my top hand rolls over sooner than this point, I will end up with a follow-through that is awkward and too low.

Just after this point, my top hand comes off the bat. This allows for a higher follow-through motion. To some, this looks funny—like I'm hitting the ball with one hand on the bat. However, as you can see, that is an illusion. My hand does not come off the bat until long after the ball is hit. Some batters prefer to keep both hands on the bat, and that is all right with me—as long as the top hand doesn't roll over too soon. If it does, they won't get that good, high follow-through. Note that my head is still emphatically down.

Here's that follow-through. My top hand continues along its natural path and finishes high
up around the head. Letting go of the bat helps
me to get that high motion, but notice that I
bring up both hands to emphasize the move.
My head? It's still down, even after the follow-
through is finished.

Some argue that taking the hand off the bat limits power. This is not so. I counted homers in the 1986 World Series between the Red Sox and the Mets, and most were slugged by hitters who took their top hand off the bat. For the Red Sox, Dwight Evans hit a couple, and his hand always comes off the bat. Dave Henderson, who in the American League Championship Series hit one of the most memorable home runs in Red Sox history, took his hand off for his World Series homers. For the Mets, little Lenny Dykstra and big Darryl Strawberry both released the bat for their home runs. The ideal finishing position is to be fully extended with a nice level swing or slightly up, with your hands high. If you can get there more easily and efficiently by releasing the bat, then drop that top hand off. The key, of course, is getting to the right position one way or another.

This isn't guesswork. We once tested Dwight Evans on a machine that measures bat speed with a laser. First we had him swing keeping both hands on the bat. Then we told him to bat his usual way and release his top hand, the way he has been doing since 1980. When he kept both hands on, the bat moved at about 45 miles per hour. When he released his top hand during the follow-through, the bat whipped along at 52 miles per hour.

There's a natural biomechanical impulse that acts to stop muscles that have been put into motion. So unless you really concentrate on the follow-through, you'll have a tendency to slow down the muscles. You'll lose speed on your follow-through, and the hit ball will actually slow down. It's very hard to keep your head down with both hands on the bat, because your top hand tends to pull you away. If you hold on to your bat, you may lose the discipline of the head that's so critical. The goal is to maintain balance for as long as you can, even after the ball has left the bat.

Keep in mind that you don't want to take your hand off the bat too soon. If you do, you'll have a tendency to move up and off the ball. Some hitters take their hand off so early that they hit one-handed. This is the danger of releasing the hand. The hand shouldn't come off until well into the follow-through, when the bat is around your front shoulder.

This isn't the easiest habit to develop, or even to believe in. Mike Greenwell, the Red Sox outfielder, is one of the smartest young hitters in baseball. He used to be unable to pull certain pitches, because he couldn't get full extension while keeping both hands on the bat. Because he's such a fine hitter, he managed to punch some of these pitches for hits. But he couldn't deposit the ball in the seats with any consistency. Mike flirted with releasing his hand from the bat for a couple of seasons before finally trusting himself to it with every swing in 1987. That year he pounded out 19 home runs in less than a full season's at-bats and drove the ball well to all fields. Obviously, Mike didn't lose any efficiency, as he still hit .328.

I've been criticized for neglecting the hips in the swing. I don't. I know the hips are important. But if you emphasize the hips too much, hitters tend to bring them into play too early. They lose the discipline of the head and wind up coming off the ball. I've found that if hitters have a proper follow-through, namely a good high finish, then their hips will come into play naturally at the proper time. The key to the hips is in the follow-through.

The final point here is that old cliché, "practice makes perfect." Every swing you take—in batting practice or in the on-deck circle—should be the exact same swing you would take in a game. I see guys waiting on deck taking swings that bear no resemblance to their game swing. What use is that? The great ones take batting practice and the on-deck circle very seriously.

It's all the rage these days to get stronger by lifting weights. But that isn't how you become a good hitter. You become a good hitter by spending your time swinging the bat the right way. Plus, it'll make you stronger. Weights aren't the answer. Nobody became a good hitter by spending three hours lifting weights and a half hour in the batting cage.

Ted Williams, one of the greatest hitters who ever lived, took more batting practice than anybody else. He hit, hit, hit until his hands bled. Carl Yastr-

A high finish is critical to a successful swing. I prefer a batter to take his top hand off the bat after making contact, but even if he holds on, I want him to keep the follow-through high. (Remember, to do that, lead with your bottom hand and roll your top hand over at the three or nine o'clock position in the circle of your swing.) These photographs show some great hitters taking their hands off the bat and some keeping their hands on. But notice that all of them finish high.

Mark McGwire

Wade Boggs

Babe Ruth

George Brett

Will Clark

Rod Carew

zemski won three batting crowns, and he took a ton of batting practice. I know because I was the guy who threw all the balls to him. He hit for hour after hour. Late in his career, as designated hitter waiting for his turn at the plate, he'd get clubhouse kids to toss him balls, and he'd hit them all over the place just to keep his stroke fine-tuned. He'd wreck the clubhouse sometimes, but he knew the importance of keeping that swing in gear.

Yastrzemski also knew that batting practice wasn't a time to fool around. If you're fooling around and not swinging right, you're doing yourself harm. You're creating bad habits that will haunt you when you go to the plate for real. You can't turn a good swing on and off. You're better off swinging right for 15 minutes and going home than spending hours in the cage swinging wrong. It's worse than a waste of time. It's detrimental to your hitting.

The Swing: Summary

1 The bottom hand is the key; the top hand provides support and should stay underneath the bat.
2 Begin the swing by starting down with the bottom hand at an angle away from the body.
3 Then move to the baseball with a nice level swing; it's OK if your swing ascends very slightly.
4 Keep the discipline of the head. That means keeping your head down until past the point of contact.
5 Watch the ball onto the bat. When you don't swing, get into the habit of watching it all the way into the catcher's mitt.
6 Try to release your hand at about three o'clock (if you're right-handed) or nine o'clock (if you're left-handed) in your swing. This is dependent on the location of the pitch.
7 Whether you release your hand or not, always finish your swing high. Practice your swing the same way every time for as long as you can.

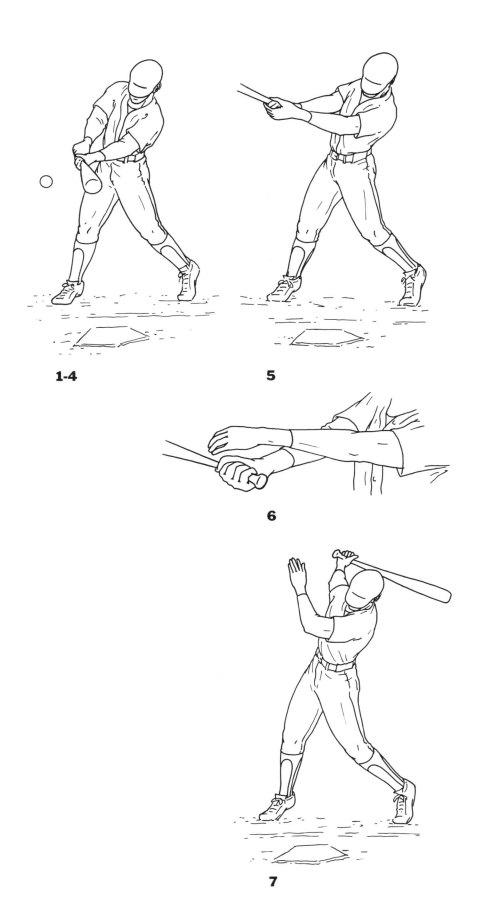

1-4

5

6

7

1

2

5

6

72

3

4

Let's review all the steps in the entire swinging sequence:

The stance (1) is the foundation of the swing. While some hitters are more straight up in their stance and shift back as the pitcher is about to release the ball, my stance begins with my weight almost all the way back and on the balls of my feet, not on my heels. My knees are bent slightly and my feet are positioned shoulder-width apart and parallel to the plate, neither open nor closed. My hands are positioned so I can get my bat quickly back to the launch position (at a 45-degree angle to the ground), and my head is aimed so I can see the pitcher clearly with both eyes.

My weight shift (2) is subtle since I'm already set back in my stance. However, some hitters find that a more definite move back works better for them. As I move back, my knees stay

bent slightly, allowing my weight to remain on the balls of my feet. My bat reaches the launch position—or very close to it—and my head remains erect for a clear view of the pitch.

Now that I'm all the way back, I begin my stride forward (3-6) to complete the weight shift. Leading with the lower half of my body, I move directly toward the pitcher. While this move is aggressive, I do not lunge. At the end of the stride, I land with my knees still bent and my front foot closed. This allows me to stay on the balls of my feet. My bat is now in the launch position, and as always, my head remains on the ball—still watching it with both eyes.

7

8

11

12

9

10

As I complete my stride, I begin my swing by bringing my bat down in a direct path to meet the ball (6-10). My weight continues to move from my back to my front side. My back heel comes off the ground and my hips are opening up (7). As my swing descends, my arms are extended with my bottom hand still leading the way. Notice my top hand; it's supporting my bottom hand, not rolling over in front of it. Still, my head remains down on the ball.

At the moment of truth (11), my weight shift is complete and my bat starts to move up. It ends with my front leg stiff and my front toe closed. My back leg is in the shape of the letter L, with my heel pointing up in the air. Most importantly, my bottom hand is still leading; my top hand has not yet rolled over. My head? It's still down on the ball.

13

14

17

18

15

16

Just after contact with the ball (12-14), I'm careful to maintain my balance. I don't fall backwards, away from the ball, and I don't pull away from the ball. I'm still leading with my bottom hand, and my top hand remains underneath. My swing continues in an upward path, and both my hands remain on the bat until approximately the nine o'clock position in my swing (15). This is the point at which my top hand rolls over my bottom hand. Just after that, I release my top hand (16). This helps me get a high finish, as well as a more fluid and efficient follow-through. Naturally, my head is still down on the ball.

My bottom hand continues in its path and finishes high up around my head (17-22). My top hand finishes high, as well. Although I obviously prefer releasing the top hand, this point is important even for batters who keep both hands on the bat. The key is to finish high —one hand or two hands. Even as the swing is complete, my head remains down, not looking up to where the ball is hit.

19

20

21

22

As I've said repeatedly, I'm a great believer in practice. This is where the critical work on hitting gets done. Once you've mastered the technique in practice, it is far easier to transfer it to a game situation. Besides regular practice, drills help a player perfect proper hitting technique. Some of these drills may seem very elementary, almost more appropriate for Little Leaguers than for professional ballplayers. But these drills help hitters break down their swing and focus on its parts.

The Flip Drill

The flip drill, or as some call it, the soft-toss drill, is fundamental. All the other drills I use are some variety of the flip drill. This drill is for everybody. The hitters who have worked with me through the years repeated this drill every single day, including such outstanding hitters as Dwight Evans, Bill Buckner, Don Baylor, Carlton Fisk, Jerry Remy, Carl Yastrzemski and Carney Lansford. They all did the flip drill religiously, no matter how well they were hitting. Dwight Evans had his best year in 1987, yet he still came out every day to perform his drills. When things are going well, we try to maintain the fluidity and proper mechanics of the swing. I see hitting as a three-part process—you start with the flip drills in the batting cage, move on to batting practice, and then sustain it in the game.

Rich Gedman and I practice the one-knee drill.

Here are some kids at my winter clinic at Tufts University doing the bottom-hand-swing and one-knee drills.

As beneficial as the flip drill is for the hitter, it can be pretty frightening for the pitcher. I'm always the pitcher. That shows how committed I am to the flip drill. I station myself about eight to ten feet directly in front of the hitter and soft-toss him a baseball. He hits just as he does in batting practice. This lets us work on all facets of hitting at a slow, relaxed pace.

The flip drill is a terrific shortcut. It removes a lot of extraneous concerns. For example, frequently the batting-practice pitcher cannot put the ball where the hitter wants it. Or perhaps no one is available to retrieve base-balls. With this drill you can concentrate on what you're trying to accomplish with the swing.

Let's say the hitter is having trouble coming off the ball—he's pulling his head up or his shoulder back, or stepping into the bucket. As a coach, I want him to recapture the feeling of hitting up the middle or to the opposite field. So in a low-key, relaxed way, without worrying about the speed of the pitch, the hitter gets to practice on easy lobs tossed over the outside half of the plate. He gets to understand, envision, and feel the opportunity to go the other way.

This helps a right-handed hitter learn how to drive the ball consistently into right field. He feels confident again—aware of what he's doing right and also of what he did wrong to get into the bad streak. The hitter can talk about and feel what's happening. He can focus on his bottom hand, his hips, his front foot, his weight shift, anything he likes. Most importantly, he can focus on the discipline of the head. He should keep his head down through the entire swing. He shouldn't follow the ball once it's hit. That's a lot easier to do in the flip drill, because the ball isn't really going anywhere anyway. There are no dramatic views of the ball soaring over the fence or even a line shot into the outfield. Once the hitter is aware of all the essential ingredients of his swing, he can transfer those positive feelings to the batting cage and, finally, to the game.

The Bottom-Hand Swing

As you know, I emphasize the importance of the bottom hand in hitting. That's the left hand for a right-handed hitter, and the right hand for a left-handed hitter. Because a lot of hitters tend to make the wrong hand dominant in the swing, I use this variation on the flip drill to correct them. I ask them to swing one-handed, with just the bottom hand. Everything else stays the same—the weight shift, the stride, the head, the follow-through. This drill increases the strength as well as the technique of the bottom hand. It helps the hitter prevent the top hand from becoming dominant and cutting off the swing.

Rich Gedman works on the bottom-hand-swing drill almost every day of the year.

The One-Knee Drill

I can see that a hitter is having problems with his swing when his hands start up instead of down. This causes a loop in the swing. Imagine that point A is the barrel of the bat, and point B is the perfect spot at which to hit the ball in front of the plate. A swing containing a loop must travel farther to get from point A to point B. The longer path not only results in an inefficient swing, but requires an earlier decision on whether or not to swing.

The one-knee drill helps eliminate the loop and get the swing on the correct path. The hitter kneels on his front knee with his rear leg extended back. The pitcher stands about four feet away at a 45-degree angle and tosses balls right at the hitter's chin. Because the pitcher is so close, the hitter, being on one knee and unable to stride, is forced to do the correct thing with his hands.

If the batter first moves his hands upward, he won't be able to get the barrel of the bat around to the ball in time. He'll wind up hitting everything on his hands, or taking it literally on the chin. The only way to get the barrel of the bat on the ball—remember, the pitcher is right on top of the hitter and there isn't much time—is to start the hands downward. The hitter will discover, courtesy of this drill, that a downward start is the quickest path to the ball. He will lose his loop or, at the very least, reduce it.

The Flat-Bat Drill

This is a more extreme measure for hitters who can't get rid of the loop. We do the flip drill, but the hitter uses a bat carved in half, keeping the flat half in position to hit the ball. If he starts his hands up in the swing—the wrong way—he'll lose the flat side of the bat and be left with hardly any hitting surface. But if he starts downward, as he's supposed to, he'll wind up with a wide hitting surface with which to club the ball.

A coach I knew invented a variation of this drill, using a stick with a basket at the end, like a lacrosse stick. If the hitter started his hands down, the basket would open up and he'd be in perfect position to catch the ball in it. But if he started the wrong way, the basket would close up and he'd be unable to catch the ball. Both drills get the hitter to recognize the correct hand movement to start his swing.

Here's another trick I sometimes use along with all these flip drills. I have the batter hit standing on the back side of the pitcher's mound, so he's facing uphill. Flip him some balls, and he'll feel his hands starting upward too soon. He'll feel the resultant loop. The swing will feel awkward and slow. Then I move him over to the front of the mound. With his front shoulder below his back shoulder, he's automatically directed downward. This lets him feel immediately how much shorter and quicker the correct swing is.

The Delay Toss

As I've explained, you have to step before you hit; you can't step and hit at the same time. A lot of hitters think that they do both at the same time, but there is always a millisecond between those two acts. I also teach hitters to lead with their bottom half—I want their top half to stay back. When hitters can't stay back, it's usually for one of two reasons. Either they're lunging at the ball, or they're stepping and hitting at the same time. Whatever the reason, the result is that the top half comes forward with the bottom half.

To correct this, I use another variation of the flip drill. I ask the hitter to take his stride. Then I hold onto the ball for another second or two before tossing it. This exaggerates the split between the stride and the swing. By turning that millisecond into a couple of seconds, the hitter gets an exaggerated feeling of first striding, and then swinging. He can then build it into his swing.

I really believe in these drills, for any hitter from Little League to the big leagues. Some people dismiss them as gimmicks, but they aren't. Gimmicks are for people who are just fooling around. These drills are no joke. They are tools to help hitters recognize and solve their hitting problems. Hitting requires correct mechanics. This means a lot of hard work and repetition as well as an understanding of the components of the swing. These drills provide that. They free the hitter in a game situation from worrying about mechanics, so he can concentrate on looking for the baseball.

Weights and Nautilus

This is not a drill per se, but the use of weight training and Nautilus equipment has been one of the most dramatic changes in baseball during the past 20 years. The Red Sox have Nautilus machines right next to the clubhouse, and some players are in there all the time. I've become a believer. Players are much stronger now than they were a couple of decades back.

However, I've seen many players get stronger but lose their upper-body flexibility. They become muscle-bound and too tight to hit. You have to be flexible to hit a baseball. Strength is not the only factor. But proper weight training or Nautilus workouts can help a player boost his strength while retaining his flexibility. Consult a physical therapist or an experienced trainer to develop an individualized workout that's just right for you. Then go to it.

There isn't a hitter alive who can cover the entire plate every time he bats. Still, you have to try to cover as much of it as possible.

Imagine the plate divided into two halves. "Middle-in" is the zone from the center of the plate toward the batter, and "middle-out" is the zone from the center of the plate away from the batter. Generally, the best way to approach the plate is to cover the middle-out zone and let the middle-in take care of itself. There are several reasons for this, but the main one is that most pitches fall into the middle-out zone. When a right-handed pitcher throws to a right-handed batter, some 70 to 80 percent of the pitches will be thrown middle-out. Fastballs can be either in or out, but almost all breaking pitches—curveballs and sliders as well as change-ups—work on the outside of the plate. The middle-out is where most of the action is. By protecting that zone, a hitter tilts the odds heavily in his favor.

By thinking middle-out, you play the pitching percentages and establish a sound hitting approach. This keeps you from trying to pull the ball all the time. Also, you are much less likely to open up in your swing. All told, it's a far sounder approach than concentrating on the inside ball. Jim Rice once told me that he feels he's close to winning the battle when pitchers start jamming him. They go inside when he controls the outside of the plate. Once Rice, or any hitter, demonstrates that he can hit up the middle or drive a good breaking pitch into the opposite field, the pitcher is the one who has to adjust. He'll try to get the hitter off the outside of the plate by pitching inside. If the hitter is thinking, he can zone middle-in and hop on the fastball.

The best way to hit is to use the whole field. Many people teach pulling the ball first, because it makes it easier to hit home runs, but pulling is one of the last things a hitter should learn. It should be thought of as a specialty that shouldn't be tackled until a hitter has mastered the basics. Look at the great hitters of the modern era. With the notable exception of Ted Williams, virtually all the current and past greats—Willie Mays, Mickey Mantle, George Brett, Don Mattingly, Rod Carew, Tony Oliva, Wade Boggs, Tim Raines, Tony Gwynn—have hit to all fields.

Pitchers will tell you they'd much rather face the guy who comes off the ball—the one who "cheats" looking for the inside pitch—than the hitter who goes straight at the baseball to protect the outside of the plate. But with some hitters, it gets to be an ego thing. They hate the look or the feel of getting jammed; they take a broken bat personally; they get infuriated by a weak dribbler or a pop-up. So they gear up for middle-in and, in effect, are willing to be beaten outside. This attitude is foolish.

Obviously, there are times to look inside, because certain pitchers throw there. Baseball is a constant guessing game. You have to take into account

the situation, the way the pitcher has pitched you before, the way he has pitched during this game. That's why managers have someone—usually the next game's starter—charting every pitch in a game. They note what pitch is thrown and where. Game situations are critical, and many pitchers will pitch one way when there is nobody on base and another way when there are runners in scoring position. Juan Marichal, the great San Francisco Giants pitcher, was a master of that. He'd give up hits when they didn't matter, but with men on, he'd really come after you. Marichal was one of those rare pitchers who could hurl a 12-hit shutout.

But back to zoning. I think that the best time to guess middle-in is after you've mastered middle-out. When you own the middle-out zone against certain pitchers and they know it, it's logical to assume that they'll come inside. Of course, certain pitchers naturally deliver inside—for example, a right-handed sinkerball pitcher facing a right-handed batter. In that case you should look for the ball inside and try to pull it, because the sinkerball tends to break inside.

Don Mattingly is typical of most great hitters in that he hits to all fields; he doesn't try to pull every pitch.

Here's another situation. The pitcher is having trouble controlling his curve. Ball one is a curve. Ball two is a curve. Strike one is a fastball. Ball three is a curve. A thinking hitter can reasonably conclude that on this day, the pitcher will resort to his fastball. It's time to zone middle-in. Wait on the fastball and try to pull it.

On such occasions, the discipline of the head is more important than ever. When you look for a pitch middle-in, you have a tendency to come off the ball, so it's especially important to concentrate on keeping your head down. Don Baylor is one of the best I know at zoning middle-in and still keeping his head on the ball. He's got tremendous discipline of the head.

I've been using the word "guess," but that's really not accurate. What we're talking about is anticipating, taking a calculated risk. To have much of a chance at the plate against the best pitchers, you almost have to take a risk. Against Roger Clemens, you'd better go up there looking fastball, because that's his main weapon. However, you must accept that if you're looking fastball and he throws a quality curve, you have no chance at all of hitting it. Still, you have a better chance to hit a curve when you're looking for a fastball than you do vice versa. You slow down a little when you're looking for a curve. If a good fastball comes, it looks as if it's steaming in at about 200 miles per hour.

The hardest task in baseball is to go to the plate and try to hit a home run. Watch batters in a home-run hitting contest. They'll take swings unlike anything they use in a game. They look totally unnatural. But there are situations—say, nobody on, two out, and a run down in the ninth—when it makes sense to try for a home run. So how do you go about that? To begin with, you should zone middle-in, because it's easier to hit a homer by pulling the ball. I'd even cheat on that by opening my stance prematurely, landing with my front toe a bit open rather than closed and trying to force the ball into my pull field. The percentages are completely against the hitter, but that's the way to go after a home run.

Many hitters find it awkward to execute a hit-and-run. That's because they're trying to change their swing for this special situation. Hitting behind the runner is simply a matter of changing your timing, not your swing. You want to hit the ball a little farther back in your swing. So you simply have to wait a little longer and hope the pitch is a good one to drive to the opposite field. Don't change your mechanics at all; the swing stays the same. But instead of trying to hit the ball out in front of you, try to hit it when it's on the plate.

A lot of baseball people talk about situation hitting—hitting ground balls to the right side to move a runner from second to third; or driving the ball in the air for a sacrifice fly to score a runner from third. Well, I'm about to commit baseball heresy. Sure, hitters should try to pull certain pitches or go the opposite way on others, but I think a hitter should try to get a hit every single time up.

If a right-handed hitter wants to move a runner from second to third, he should swing late. But he shouldn't go into contortions trying to produce a ground ball to the right side. Go for the base hit. If you fail to get a hit, you've managed to make an out on the right side of the field and advance the runner. But I don't believe a hitter should ever "give himself up." That's defeatist thinking. Moreover, it too often fails. The same concept applies when trying to lift the ball for a sacrifice fly. If a guy with a perfectly good swing, who practices that swing day in and day out, suddenly tries a new swing that he uses about 10 times a year, he might get the ball in the air. But I figure it's just as likely that he'll pop up as hit a sacrifice fly.

It's very tough to hit when you have to think about swinging one way on inside pitches, another way on outside pitches, and a third way with runners in position. My philosophy is not to compromise sound hitting mechanics in an attempt to score a single run. Truly great hitters can make adjustments for game situations, or even for certain ballparks or playing conditions. Boggs, for example, sometimes takes advantage of a wind blowing out to right field by adjusting his swing and putting a little lift into it. But few hitters are good enough to make minor adjustments in each at-bat, or even in each game, without messing up their overall swing. Boggs is really an exception. He can tell me, "Walter, I'm going to hit like this tonight," and he does it.

For most hitters, I emphasize zoning middle-out first. Change to middle-in only when you think you've forced the pitcher to come inside. But don't zone middle-in too often.

Middle-out positions you best for the curveball, for the slider, for the change-up, and for the fastball outside. The only ball that might give you real trouble is the fastball inside. Thus, percentages are hugely in favor of middle-out. Sometimes you can make those percentages even greater by moving up in the batter's box. When you face a pitcher who throws mostly off-speed stuff, it helps to move forward in the batter's box and try to catch his stuff before it breaks too much.

All this should be disregarded when you have two strikes. In that situation, forget about zoning, and protect the plate. The plate has suddenly become much bigger. You can't chance letting a ball go that seems an inch or so outside or inside, low or high; the umpire might call you out.

So up until two strikes, you should zone constantly and look for certain pitches. With two strikes, the only zone you should worry about is the strike zone—which has expanded. You shouldn't guess; just look for the baseball. Switch from being an aggressive, offensive hitter to being a defensive hitter. Consider choking up on the bat, shortening the swing a little, or not swinging as hard.

The best hitters often seem to flick at tough two-strike pitches in order to foul them off. Nobody's a better hitter with two strikes on him than Wade Boggs, which is why he's willing to take two strikes looking for the pitch he wants. With two strikes, he'll concentrate on protecting the plate, often fouling off strike after strike until the pitcher slips and delivers one in his prime hitting zone.

Dwight Evans

Evans on Hriniak: The year was 1980, my eighth full season with the Red Sox. I had just signed a nice contract, I was in great shape—and I was having the worst year of my career. I was hitting .180 or .190. I was an easy out. "What's going on here?" I kept asking myself.

I was always trying something different. I'd have a stance for a week, and then I'd have another stance for another week. Open, closed, down low, stand up straight. I was known as The Man of a Thousand Stances. They'd all work for a period of time, but there was no consistency in my stance or in my life. They go hand in hand. I was lost, and desperate. Walt asked me, "You want to try something?" I told him the truth: "Anything!"

Walter came to me at the right time. Nobody really wanted to work with me the way Walter was willing to. He knew a lot about hitting, but I don't think he had worked out all the little details yet. And I'm not sure he had figured out how to teach what he knew. As great as it was for me to have him, it was pretty good for him to have me, too. We learned an awful lot together. Walter is an extremely hardworking man. He's the kind of hitting instructor who can help any hitter. Look at Bill Buckner, who, after 2,000 hits in the majors, adopted Walt's weight shift and high finish. That really tells you something.

Anyway, back in 1980 Walter offered me this business about the weight shift and keeping your head down. A lot of people are confused by that. They think that when Walt says, "Put your head down," it means put your head down over the plate. He's not suggesting that. What he means is, put your head where you hit the ball. A lot of great hitters do it without even realizing it. Some hitters talk about getting their hips into it, but that's not the main point. The main point is where your head should be. The discipline of the head is what's really essential.

Walter and I talked over this theory. The weight shift was the big thing that I had to adjust to. Until then I had primarily been a stand-still hitter—no shift at all. Now I am a total believer. That's another thing a lot of great hitters do without understanding or even realizing it. Walter has pictures of Babe Ruth that show him shifting from back side to front side. Henry Aaron also had great natural weight shift.

Walter and I have been working on this ever since. It's constant maintenance. We have a little saying, the two of us: "Every time you do it right it's like taking a penny and putting it in the bank." The more times you do it, the more pennies you've banked, the more you're going to have it down. You can work on something for a solid month—say, keeping your head down—and have it going perfectly, but it only takes a couple of days of sloppy work to undo it.

It's all discipline. Repetition is part of that discipline. Over and over and over. I can't tell you how many swings I've taken since 1980. Every day, with no off days. That includes during the season. There are some days during the season when you're tired and you feel you couldn't possibly get loose, but you go out there and do it anyway. And it pays off. You have to maintain that swing; you can lose it so quickly.

There's another interesting sidelight to the weight shift. Before I worked with Walt and adopted the weight shift, I had been beaned three times. In 1978 I was hit in the head, and I had an inner-ear problem for over two years. I rarely fell asleep at night without rolling over and getting nauseous and dizzy. I never realized how flat-footed and off-balance I was at the plate, and thus how much I was at the mercy of the pitcher. When I adopted the weight shift, I found that I was far more balanced in my stance and could get out of the way of the ball with far greater ease. I don't worry about getting beaned anymore. I know I can get out of the way. Sure, you might get hit, but you're unlikely to get hurt.

When the whole swing is going right, it seems effortless. But what's re-markable to me is that when I do it right, my bat speed is at least five or

Dwight Evans

six miles per hour quicker, which is really significant when you're looking for power. Many critics of Walter's teaching say he advocates a swing that produces only line drives—a base-hit swing that isn't geared for power. I think that's because so many of Walt's students have not inherently been home-run hitters. But it's definitely helped my home-run production. I became one of the leading home-run hitters in all of baseball once I began swinging this way back in 1980.

Hriniak on Evans: Dwight Evans has become a better hitter with age. His success is the result of the changes he made beginning in 1980 and the tremendous effort he has put forth since then. I remember watching Dwight when I first came up with the Red Sox in 1977. He had had respectable years—say, 24 homers, 63 RBIs—years like that. He'd show some streaks of tremendous hitting, but there was no consistency. He'd change stances, he'd change thoughts, he'd change everything. People said Dwight Evans had great potential, but he never seemed to put it together.

I'll never forget when it all began for the two of us. It was just before the All-Star break in 1980, and we were playing in Baltimore. Dwight was hitting .180 and had pretty much lost his regular job to Jimmy Dwyer. He was at the low point of his career. On July 5, 1980, he came to me and said he wanted some help. I said, "Fine. But you have to decide that you won't change once we make up our minds about what we're going to do." That was the challenge I gave him.

We started that very day with the flip drill in the batting cage. We took it one step at a time. Otherwise, it's just too much for anyone. I always start with the head—the discipline of the head is number one. Even when I'm teaching something else, I reinforce that lesson. Some of the other things I teach aren't absolutes, just techniques to accomplish something desirable. For example, you can get excellent extension and your hands high without releasing the top hand off the bat. Ellis Burks is a good example of that. But Dwight adopted the whole package step by step.

It was a real struggle for him, because the changes were so drastic. He was changing from being a still hitter to a hitter who moves around the plate. He was trying to work out a pendulum swing with the bat to time the pitcher. He was moving his feet back and forth for rhythm and balance, and he was working on a little jab-step backward to get his weight back. At the same time, he was going from his set of open and closed stances to a square stance at the plate every time up. Here was a guy who bailed out trying to hit every pitch thrown to him in Fenway over the left-field wall. Now he was trying to stride directly toward the pitcher, keeping his front toe closed in order to hit everything up the middle.

Another hitting habit he had never acquired was putting his head down on the ball and not watching it when it left the bat. Plus, he was learning to release his top hand off the bat, another hitting technique he'd never tried before. He took a lot of grief from the sidelines. When he released his hand, people would say, "What are you doing? You're hitting the ball one-handed!" Both of us knew that wasn't the case. But Dwight was under all this pressure because he was changing everything in midseason. He not only had to change; he had to learn to believe in those changes.

The commitment he was willing to make at that time in his career—after all, he was a respected veteran—showed an extraordinary amount of courage. It was hard enough to do these things in batting practice, let alone go out there in game situations and try to get a hit. There were some slumps when we both became skeptical whether it would ever work. I remember a couple of times when Dwight was fed up and questioning the whole thing. He wanted to make some changes. I told him, "If you want to change, go ahead, but don't ever come back."

I took that hard line because I knew the biggest problem Dwight had as a hitter—one shared by many others—was that he experimented too much at the plate and made too many changes. I was trying hard to make sure that he didn't give up on those things that I knew would work. There will always be tough times, but you make a commitment and ride out the slumps. That's the professional, commonsense way to be successful. Obviously, it worked for Dwight. Since 1980 he's been a consistent good-average hitter with plenty of power. If the Red Sox had won the pennant again in 1987, Dwight might have found himself MVP. To hit over .300 with 34 home runs and 123 RBIs is the stuff of superstars.

This technique is not something Dwight learned in 1980 and has had down pat ever since. He comes to the ballpark every day to work on his swing and make minor adjustments. Since 1980, he's missed working out at the ballpark only four or five times a year. Every day he does the drills, every day some extra hitting. Every swing he takes is a conscious effort to create what we want. Every swing should be perfect. The aim of all this practice is to create the right mental and physical process at the plate. Batting practice is not a tool to get loose; you can do that lifting weights.

Dwight Evans takes batting practice as well as anyone I've ever seen. He comes to the ballpark more than three hours before a game. We work together for a while; if he's going good, only for about 10 minutes. Then he takes his regular batting practice, for another 5 minutes. Sometimes we'll work on drills, or he'll take a little more extra hitting.

Today Dwight uses the whole park from foul line to foul line. Once a guy who pulled everything, he can now hit a single up the middle or a home run to right field. Dwight is also among the leaders in walks every season. During that great 1987 season, he managed to lead the league in walks with 106. Couple that with a .305 average and you have a sensational .417 on-base percentage. All those walks are a result of his hitting technique. Once Dwight began to think differently at the plate, he acquired more discipline in his overall approach to hitting. By looking to go up the middle, you don't have to commit your swing as early. Waiting a little longer lets you watch the ball longer, and you can lay off more bad pitches. As you learn to hit, you also learn to walk.

Dwight Evans is an example of a hitter getting the most out of himself. His age doesn't matter. Any hitter who wants to improve himself, whether he's 18 or 40, can do so by making the necessary changes. But he has to have the desire, and he'd better not be afraid of hard work. That's the other thing I told Dwight when he first came to me: You're going to have to work your butt off. He did just that and has never stopped. Now it's the only way he knows to go about his business. It's become his style. He can't get ready to play a game any other way, and he'll continue that way until the day he quits baseball.

Wade Boggs

Boggs on Hriniak: Most of what I want to say about Walter I've put in the introduction to this book. However, there are some more points I want to make. Some people say Walter's theories are for line-drive hitters. For example, there's been a lot of talk about whether or not I should hit for power. I've got all the power in the world, and I'm proving I can hit home runs, so it's really a question of whether I want to hit line drives or fly balls. I see line drives as coming from a perfect swing. They feel better to me. With fly balls, there's a lot of room for error. What I've always tried to do by hitting line drives is to cut down on the possibility of making a mistake. That way I cut down on the possibility of making an out.

I want to add that I don't think little kids should worry about all these things. The discipline, the weight shift, all this theory shouldn't start until the teenage years. Little Leaguers should just go out there, keep their heads down, and watch the ball. When you get to be 13 or so, you can start getting serious. Before that, follow my example and get out there and play the game. If you can't get a game, play pepper. That's a great game, and it only takes two people. One guy throws and one guy hits. Just keep your head down on the ball and concentrate on making good contact.

Hriniak on Boggs: Wade Boggs is the greatest hitter I've ever seen. In 1987, he added another dimension to his swing—the ability to hit home

Wade Boggs

runs. He's always had the power, but he waited to establish himself as a truly great hitter before he began looking for opportunities to aim for home runs. Up till now, only three players had higher lifetime averages than Boggs—Ty Cobb, Rogers Hornsby, and Shoeless Joe Jackson. Now Wade is a home-run threat to boot. He can begin to think in terms of a .370 average and a 30-home-run season.

I think that's a great goal for Wade. Mickey Mantle came close, but never managed it. Hank Aaron never did it. Willie Mays never did it. The guys who did were few and far between, hitters like Babe Ruth, Lou Gehrig, Joe DiMaggio, Stan Musial, and Ted Williams. No one has done it since 1957, when Ted Williams hit .388 and slugged 38 home runs at age 39. Forget the home runs. Only Rod Carew (.388 in 1977), George Brett (.390 in 1980), and Tony Gwynn (.370 in 1987) have hit as high as .370 since then.

Before Gwynn it had been almost four decades—back to Stan Musial in 1948—since anyone had hit that high in the National League.

Wade has been a great help to me when it comes to teaching hitting. He's a great model for the things I teach. The thing that separates Wade from all the rest is his ability to lower his head on the baseball, and keep it down and still. Whenever players come to me and want to learn this hitting technique, I tell them to watch Wade, because he has mastered the discipline of the head.

A writer from New York once asked me, "What's this thing you're trying to teach about the head?" I said, "Tonight when you're watching the game, pay particular attention to Wade Boggs at the plate. When he swings the bat, don't watch the ball, regardless of whether it's a line drive, a home run, or a foul pop-up. Keep your eye on Wade's head and tell me what you see during and after his swing. Then when you see what he does, watch what the other hitters do, particularly those on the other team."

When the game was over, the writer came over and said, "Wade Boggs keeps his head down after he's hit the ball, longer than most of the other hitters. A lot of your guys on the Red Sox keep their heads there, but the other team's heads are seldom there." I told him, "That's what I mean about the discipline of the head."

Wade has a balanced, workable stance. He doesn't get back in his stance like Evans, but he definitely gets back before he swings. He includes a weight shift in his stance. If you watch his front leg, you'll see his right knee turn in a little, much the way Ted Williams cocked his leg, which pushes his weight back. Then he makes a positive, aggressive move forward with his front leg.

Wade always lands closed—never open—keeping himself balanced and square to the baseball. He has excellent awareness of leading with his lower half, keeping his top half back in the launching position. As a result, he lands in an extremely strong hitting position. Then, a millisecond later, his bat comes forward into the strike zone. His hands start downward, and by the time he gets to that ideal spot to make contact, his bat angle is level or slightly up. At the moment of contact, his head is down over the baseball, and remains down longer than anyone in baseball.

He has a tremendous follow-through, though sometimes in practice I think he has an even better one by releasing his top hand. But in the game he usually hangs on with two hands. However, he gets his hands high, up around his ears. He doesn't just beat on the ball and roll his top hand over. He continues the swing and gets excellent follow-through with both hands finishing high.

Now add to that perfect stance, stride, swing, and an incredible mental attitude toward the game. Much has been written about how Wade eats chicken all the time. That isn't the only consistency in his life. He makes some sort of cross in the batter's box before he gets into it, he takes ground balls at precisely the same time every day, and he runs at the same time— exactly seven minutes and 17 seconds before the start of the game.

A lot of writers and other baseball folk treat this as amusing superstition. But I see it as far more. It's part of a regimented, disciplined way to get ready to play the game. Wade prepares for baseball every day, mentally as well as physically. And he's always looking for ways to get better. He's never satisifed. Boggs came into the league with a reputation as a weak defensive player, but through hard work he has made himself one of the best fielding third basemen in baseball. That's hard work, and discipline.

Wade also has tremendous discipline in the strike zone. He has such confidence at the plate that he feels he can wait for the pitch that he wants to hit. He's not afraid to take one or even two strikes waiting for his pitch. Then, if it still doesn't come, he'll foul strike after strike until he finds one to his liking.

I appreciate the credit Wade has given me for his success, but I don't feel I've done that much at all. I certainly haven't changed him. What I have done is point out those things he does well and try to make sure he continues doing them. For example, I'd watch him swing with his head was usually right on the ball; but sometimes in batting practice I'd see his head move. So I tried to make him aware of how important the discipline of the head is in batting practice to help him carry it over into the game more easily.

I also worked with Wade on pulling the ball more. His best swing was from left field to center, and I knew that sooner or later the opposition was going to pitch him in a way that he'd be forced to pull the ball. So we worked on that a lot in practice.

About the only thing I haven't been able to convince Wade is that he should bunt more. Wade can bunt; I've seen him do it in practice. He gets out of the box quickly and has good speed to first base. Bunting would be a terrific additional weapon in his arsenal. But Wade isn't comfortable with the idea. He says, "I feel like if I bunt, I'm giving up." That's how good he is—he thinks he can get a hit every time up. If I could convince him to bunt in certain situations, it would make him even better. The year Carew hit .388, I think he had 28 bunt singles. If Wade decided to bunt, he'd be an even more serious threat to hit .400.

Carney Lansford

Lansford on Hriniak: I spent three years in the major leagues with California before coming to the Red Sox in a trade in 1981. I'd never had a hitting instructor who was willing to spend the amount of time with an individual that Walter did. I went to him on the advice of Joe Rudi, the former Oakland star who came to the Red Sox in the same trade. Joe knew what kind of hitting instructor Walter was. I figured it was an opportunity I couldn't afford to miss, so I approached him immediately at the beginning of spring training.

We started working together in the batting cage from day one, and we worked every day for the next two years until I was traded to Oakland. Walt picked apart my stance and started me with the basics. The main thing he drilled into me was to keep my head down on every swing and not to pull off the ball. That's been the biggest thing that's helped me. It's the single biggest problem most hitters have. They don't keep their head down the entire time. Usually they pull off at the very last second, which is the most important time to keep your head on the ball. I've always remembered that lesson, and I've worked on it so long now that it's a habit for me.

Besides keeping my head down, Walt worked on getting me to stay back and to use the entire field. We worked day in and day out on driving the ball to right field. It paid off. I think 80 percent of my hits in 1981 were to the right of second base, and I won the batting title with a .336 average— up 75 points from the year before. I was the first right-handed hitter to win the American League batting crown since Alex Johnson won it in 1970. Obviously, all that work really paid off.

After I left the Red Sox, I missed having Walter there to pick up on little things I might be doing wrong. I get into some bad habits sometimes. Walter would pick them up immediately and keep me out of longer slumps. He had that special knack. He knew every detail of your stance and your swing because he put so much effort into his job and worked so hard with the players. He could spot a mistake instantly, and that's what keeps you out of those bad slumps.

I tell young ballplayers to listen to Walt and take what he says seriously. Develop good hitting habits and practice them every day. Good habits in practice will turn into good habits during the game. What you do in workouts and batting practice really does carry over into the real games. That's how I wound up with a batting title.

Hriniak on Lansford: Carney was one of the most enjoyable people I ever worked with as a hitting instructor. When he asked for some help, I took him out to the batting cage and started with some flip drills. I was showing him all the stuff about getting back and holding your bat a certain way and

Carney Lansford

this and that, and it seemed to me that he was getting a little frustrated. So I told him, "If there's something here that we're working on that you don't particularly like or that you don't think you can handle, speak up."

He did speak up. There were just too many changes for him. Carney finally agreed to try two fundamental changes in his approach to hitting. The first was to always keep his head down. The second was to try to hit every ball right back at the pitcher. I told him, "You've got six weeks in spring training, and I want you to try these two things every time you swing a bat. I want 100 percent effort with every swing. Then, right before the end of spring training, you can decide whether you think these things are valuable or not."

Carney was already doing a lot of things right. He cocked his front leg to get his weight back, and he moved his hands around to keep from freezing as the pitch was thrown. So I just wanted to work on those two critical things. We started working in the cage every day. Carney put a piece of paper on the ground at approximately the spot he'd be hitting the baseball, to give him something to focus on and make sure he kept his head down after hitting the ball. I've gone on to use that technique with a lot of other players. As you teach, you can still learn from your players. Coaches should never let their egos get so big that they close their minds to new ideas.

I threw extra batting practice for Carney every day, and he tried to drill every ball right back at me. Sometimes I couldn't get the ball in the right spot for him. I'd be all over the place, inside and outside, and he'd get frustrated. But he never changed his approach. He kept coming right back at me with his head down.

A bottom-line approach doesn't tell you everything about this game, but numbers like .336 don't lie. Perhaps more impressive than his average that year was how he cut down on his strikeouts. In his two years with California, Carney had struck out 115 and 93 times, respectively. In 1981 in 102 games (that was the strike-shortened season), he struck out just 28 times. At that rate, over a full season, he would have had only about 45 strikeouts. That means Carney cut his strikeouts by more than half. That's pretty good testimony that he was seeing the ball a whole lot better once he started keeping his head down. Carney is a prime example of how a couple of changes can make all the difference in the world.

I tell Carney's story every year at my hitting school, because the most important thing you can help someone to do is watch the ball. If you watch the ball just a bit longer, you'll hit it more often and get more hits. You'll also swing at fewer bad pitches, so you'll walk more and strike out less.

But people are always looking to put a rap on the hitter. It wasn't enough for Carney to hit .336. Like Boggs after him, people began saying that Carney couldn't hit home runs. I told them, "In time, he'll add the home runs too." Obviously, if Carney is looking to hit everything up the middle, he's not looking for home runs or to pull the ball over the shortest part of the fence. But once you learn the discipline of the head, you can learn how to do that same thing out in front a little bit more and pull the ball. It's just a question of relocating your head a little bit farther out in front and looking for the inside pitch to pull. In his years at Oakland, Carney has proved me right. He has kept his average up, though not quite as high as it had been in Boston, *and* he has boosted his home runs quite a bit. Like Boggs, he has added another dimension to his already considerable hitting skills.

I love watching baseball. Besides the exhibition games and the 162 regular-season games, I watch baseball on television whenever I can. Mostly I study the hitters. Here are some of my favorites. If I'm a little biased toward American League hitters, it's only because I get to see them far more often. I'm sure I'd become a fan of Tony Gwynn, Eric Davis, and Benito Santiago if I got to see them play more regularly.

The Veterans

George Brett

If there are a dozen pieces to the hitting puzzle, George fits each and every one of those pieces. He's off the plate, he moves around in the batter's box, he gets back, he strides and lands with the front toe closed, he doesn't try to pull the ball all the time, he keeps to the middle of the field, and he releases the top hand off the bat on every swing. George Brett is a textbook hitter.

Brett didn't hit like that in the minor leagues. He didn't lower his head, he didn't get back, and he didn't release his top hand. If you go back and check his minor-league record, you'll find that he didn't hit .330 or .340; more like

George Brett

.270 or .280. He learned to hit properly in the majors, and much of the credit goes to Charlie Lau, who was George's hitting coach at Kansas City. It took a while—some two or three years—before George fully adapted to this style of hitting. It didn't come easily. But he had the desire and the commitment to stick to it, and he just got better and better.

The thing about George that stood out when I first saw him was his awareness of his head. He never watched the ball leave the bat. He kept his head down completely throughout the swing. Sometimes he almost looked as if he was fighting to keep it down. A couple years later I noticed he had lost some of that discipline. He started picking up his head and watching the ball. Maybe there was a little pressure on him to try to hit home runs. I once asked him why he was doing that when he had worked so hard at keeping his head down previously. He said, "Oh, that's why I'm hitting .310 instead of .350."

Dave Winfield

Dave is one of the outstanding hitters in the game. I especially like the way he stays off the plate so he can go to right field. Dave uses the entire field, which makes him a home-run threat from foul line to foul line. Look at the way he starts his bat movement. He starts it down, which enables him to

Dave Winfield

maintain a short, compact swing. That gives him a great hitting advantage. Sometimes he looks a little wild, but if you slow his swing down on tape, you'll see that he manages to get his head down at the moment of contact. Also, he has excellent follow-through, taking his top hand off the bat after contact. All in all, Winfield is one terrific ballplayer, especially when you add his defensive and base-running skills.

Mike Schmidt

Here's another sure Hall of Famer. A guy who has hit more than 500 home runs must be doing a lot of things right. What I love about Mike is that he has made so many adjustments throughout his career. About five or six years ago, he backed off the plate a little bit to give himself more room. That enabled him to get more extension and go to right field more often. He hits many more home runs to center field and right field than he used to.

Mike has great rhythm in his stance. Watch him carefully, and you'll see him shake his legs a little right before he goes to the ball. That movement in his stance relieves the tension and lets him relax and take a smooth swing at the ball. Home-run hitters have a tendency to overswing because they're going for the long ball, and often they come out of themselves or unravel a

Mike Schmidt

bit more than contact hitters like Pete Rose or Tony Gwynn. But Mike's little shake in his legs is a mechanism that allows him to stay within himself, to keep the rhythm throughout his entire swing.

Mike has a lovely, compact swing. He doesn't try to muscle the ball out of the park. He starts his hands down, keeps his swing short, and doesn't have an uppercut. The only criticism I can muster is that his top hand is a little too dominant, but it sure has worked for him.

Jim Rice

Jim had a tough act to follow in left field for the Red Sox—two legends: Ted Williams and Carl Yastrzemski. We know Carl is going to join Ted in the Hall of Fame at his first opportunity, and I think Jim Rice will get there, too. A career .300 hitter who's on his way to 400 career home runs, nobody has knocked in more runs or had more total bases over the past decade. In 1978, he had one of the most incredible seasons ever, compiling 406 total bases, and was voted Most Valuable Player in the American League. Only 15 hitters ever totaled more bases than that, and 14 of them did it before 1938. The only other post-war hitter to total that many bases was Stan Musial back in 1948. Since then, Jim's season stands alone.

Jim Rice

One of the most remarkable things about Jim is that such a tremendously strong guy has been able to resist the temptation of the left-field wall in Fenway Park. It's a tribute to his discipline that he doesn't try to pull the ball exclusively. The last few years he's had a lot of success going to right. A lot of good hitters have failed miserably in Fenway because they changed their batting style to try to take advantage of the wall. I once asked Rice what he thought his lifetime average would have been if he had tried to pull everything. He said, "Probably .240 or .250."

Jim starts the bat down and has a good short swing. He has excellent discipline of the head, keeping on the ball. He also lands square to the baseball; he doesn't spin out at all. That's because he doesn't try to force the ball toward left field. If he were trying to pull everything, you'd see him spin out and land with his front toe open. His hips would open too fast, and his head would leave the ball. But he's simply too knowledgeable a hitter to do that.

Players In Their Prime

Jesse Barfield

Barfield is establishing himself as one of the premier players in the game. He's outstanding defensively, and his throwing arm ranks with the very best of the modern era, Dwight Evans and Roberto Clemente. Injuries caused a disappointing season in 1988; still, he's a dynamite hitter.

Jesse has a very good stance and excellent mechanics in his swing. If you watch him closely before the pitch is thrown, he'll do a little sit-back on his back leg—that's his way of getting back. He usually has good discipline of the head, when he's hitting well and in a good groove. Occasionally, when he's slumping, you'll see him pull his head off the ball too fast. He doesn't always release his top hand, but even when he hangs on he gets good extension. He doesn't cut the swing off with that top hand. He uses his bottom hand correctly and gets his hand through the ball. He has the proper extension, resulting in an excellent high finish to his swing.

George Bell

There are many similarities between Barfield and his running mate in the Toronto outfield, George Bell. The most obvious one is that he's brutal on American League pitchers. He followed his .309, 31-home-run, 108-RBI season in 1986 with an MVP season in 1987 and a solid, if a little disappointing, 1988. He has established himself among the handful of most feared hitters in the league.

Bell looks a lot like Barfield at the plate. He starts out in a nice balanced stance, with his weight distributed equally front and back. Just before the pitcher delivers the ball, he'll do that same little sit-back in his legs. As I've said repeatedly, it's essential to get that weight shift back, and George and Jesse do it their own way. For a home-run hitter, he doesn't try to pull the ball all the time, but makes good use of the whole field.

The only problem I see is that he doesn't always have good extension. Sometimes, when the ball is in on him, he seems to cut off his swing. He seems to get locked up. But even when he's locked up, he can still muscle the ball into left field. When the ball is out over the plate, he gets great extension, releasing his top hand and frequently hitting the ball into right field. Sometimes it seems he has two completely different swings.

Kirby Puckett

Kirby is testimony to how a seemingly small change can bring incredible results. Nothing we saw of this guy in 1985 indicated that he was anything more than a good solid hitter with a fair amount of speed, but almost no power. Maybe I could have foreseen that he would boost his average the next year by 40 points. But I never imagined that he would go from 4 home runs to 31.

Jesse Barfield

George Bell

What happened? Basically, Kirby learned how to shift his weight back. He adopted that rare front-leg lift that the great Mel Ott employed to hit more than 500 home runs. Very few hitters use it, because although it shifts the weight back, maintaining good balance becomes very difficult. About the only other hitters using it very successfully now are White Sox outfielder Harold Baines and Texas Ranger shortstop Scott Fletcher, who has quietly put together some fine seasons. Tony Oliva, who was a three-time batting champ with the Twins and is now their hitting coach, taught Puckett the move. Kirby's version has an extremely high kick. The lift shifts his weight back before he goes forward and gives him a lot more power in his swing.

Tim Raines

As I said, I don't get to watch the National League hitters as much as I do those in the American League, but one guy who has always impressed me is Tim Raines. I like the way he stands in the batter's box—he's off the plate and always going toward the ball. He always tries to hit up the middle and has good weight shift. Tim keeps his head down and releases his top hand for proper extension. I'd like to see more of him; he generates a lot of excitement when he comes to the plate. In 1986 he had a .413 on-base percentage and stole 70 bases. Tim had another spectacular year in 1987 before slumping in 1988.

Kirby Puckett

Tim Raines

Harold Baines

Harold is another student of Charlie Lau. He uses the leg lift like Kirby Puckett, and he has a really good weight-shift. He gets forward in a hurry. Sometimes he gets there too fast and winds up hitting too much on his front side. But because he keeps excellent discipline of the head, he can compensate for such mistakes.

I can't overemphasize the discipline of the head. Once you're committed to the weight shift, sometimes your timing will be imperfect. More often, you'll get caught forward rather than back. To operate successfully, you have to make sure that your head is still there on the ball. If you lose the discipline of the head, you'll be too far forward and coming off the ball at the same time. You'll be helpless up there. When Harold gets caught forward, he might not be able to hit a home run, but he still can flick a single or a double. He can still operate the bat. Getting caught too far forward is a problem, but Baines is one of the best at not compounding the mistake. He keeps his head down and stays dangerous.

Joe Carter

A fine ballplayer. He has a nice, balanced stance, but the thing that distinguishes Joe is his short, quick swing. He achieves that by starting not on

Harold Baines

Joe Carter

the upswing, but on the downswing. He keeps two hands on the bat all the way, but he can make a good follow-through and get his hands up. Carter has good discipline of the head. Despite his power, he doesn't try to pull the ball all the time. He uses the whole field. He's already a member of the 30-30 club (30 home runs and 30 steals), and is definitely one of the up-and-coming stars of the league.

Darryl Strawberry

Darryl has a lot of good hitting attributes, but he really stands out in one area. He has tremendous extension, which he accomplishes by releasing the bat with his top hand on every swing. Some hitters only manage that occasionally; they release the bat properly when the ball is out over the plate, but when it's inside they hang on with two hands and try to muscle the ball. Darryl releases the top hand no matter where the pitch is. As a result, he's a home-run threat on every pitch. Bill Robinson, the excellent hitting coach of the Mets, is trying to get Strawberry to use left field more. I think Darryl will eventually be able to hit consistently to all fields.

Don Mattingly

We've saved the best for last in this category. Next to Wade Boggs, Don Mattingly is the greatest hitter in the game today. Their paths were very

Darryl Strawberry

Don Mattingly

similar. When Mattingly came up, he was a high-average hitter with little power. He found he could retain the average while hitting for power a couple years before Wade did. The two of them will dominate the league for the next decade. Mattingly has a little more power and a better park for his power, and Wade will dominate the batting championships and steadily improve his power statistics. But they share a common destination—the Hall of Fame.

Don learned this little move to get his weight back: Just before the pitcher throws the ball, he squats back on his left foot. That's the key to his hitting technique. Everything else he does follows the classic technique we've discussed. He has a terrific weight shift, keeps his head down, and has fine extension. What I can't teach is his great attitude. He has a tremendous outlook and is driven to succeed.

The Kids

Mark McGwire

This big kid sure surprised the baseball world with his early record-breaking home-run pace. I had some inkling of McGwire's talents when Tony La-

Mark McGwire

Russa, the Oakland Athletics manager, told me at the beginning of the 1987 season to keep my eye on Mark. I watched. His stance may look a bit unorthodox, but fundamentally it appears to be sound and balanced. His head is in a good position, and he gets it down on the ball pretty well. He also has a good finish, completing his swing with his hands extremely high and sometimes, particularly when he's going to the opposite field, releasing the top hand off the bat.

The only problem I've seen with McGwire is he sometimes swings drastically upward. Even then he made his swing workable, loop and all. But with this kind of swing, he becomes vulnerable to high fastballs. This seems to contradict the old adage—"keep the ball down to power hitters." But keeping the ball down is the worst thing you can do with certain hitters. If you have a loop in your swing, it's a lot easier to hit a ball that is down than a high, hard one. In fact, if you have an uppercut, you'll have real trouble hitting a high pitch unless it's a change-up. With a ball down low, you don't have to be as quick.

Jose Canseco

Jose is the other fist in the one-two punch of the Oakland Athletics and the 1988 MVP. He uses the whole field, and he can really power the ball out to

Jose Canseco

right field. For a guy who takes a hard swing, he has excellent discipline of the head. If you watch him closely, you'll see that even when he doesn't swing he follows the ball back into the catcher's glove, just like Wade Boggs. That's an outstanding habit. He starts the bat down, not up, and has a nice, short swing, with decent extension. I really like the way Jose hits, and I think he has the ability not only to hit 30 to 40 home runs a year for a long time, but to be a consistent .300 hitter as well.

Wally Joyner

Wally reminds me a lot of Fred Lynn when he first came up with the Red Sox. He's a subtle hitter who never seems to take too hard a swing. Wally is always under control. His stance is nice and balanced. Like all the others I've talked about, he uses the whole field.

The players I've cited obviously have a lot in common. One thing they share is the ability to use the whole field. It doesn't matter whether they're right-handed or left-handed, whether they're contact hitters or power hitters; using the whole field gives the hitter such an obvious advantage. Only a hitter of the caliber of Ted Williams can consistently pull the ball, defy a shift that puts three men on the right side of the infield, and still hit a high average.

Wally Joyner

Wally is not your classic home-run hitter. He's not big and strong like the Oakland kids, but he hits home runs as a result of excellent technique. His weight shift and extension are most notable. Watch Joyner finish his swing. He takes his top hand off the bat at the proper time. As I said before, the bottom line is to finish with your hands high. There are different ways to get that extension. If you can't do it with both hands on the bat, take a lesson from Joyner and release the top hand.

Mike Greenwell

This young man has a lot going for him at the plate. He has excellent work habits and mechanics, and a very aggressive, live bat. Sometimes he's a little too aggressive and swings too hard. As a result, Mike's head occasionally flies off the ball. But he's shown excellent ability to make adjustments.

When Mike first came up, he was pulling the ball too much. First he moved off the plate a little, so he wouldn't get jammed up too often. Then he worked hard on the discipline of the head, so he could take a longer look at the ball. Waiting longer helped keep him from overswinging. Finally, he improved his extension by learning to take his hand off the bat consistently. That really made things smoother for Mike. By the end of his first full season in the majors, he had learned to drive the ball all over the park.

Mike Greenwell

No matter how gifted an athlete is, he will not become a great hitter by relying only on his physical abilities. The mental approach to the game is critical. It takes extraordinary discipline and self-control to make yourself the best player you can be. The only place to do that is in practice. Practice is not a warm-up for the real game. It is an extension of the game; it is the place to develop the habits that you want to display when the game begins.

Baseball is one of the most demanding of all sports when it comes to mental discipline. There is a tremendous amount of failure in baseball; even the best hitters are successful only about 3 out of every 10 times at the plate. In football, a quarterback completing only 30 percent of his passes would be booed off the field. A basketball player who shot 30 percent would never last as a pro. A tennis player who landed only 30 percent of his first serves wouldn't make it past the first round of any tournament. But in baseball, great athletes must adjust to failing most of the time.

And that's when things are going well. When things are going badly, it can seem intolerable. All of a sudden, a hitter can't buy a base hit. For a game, for a week. He becomes overly conscious of every aspect of his body and his swing. He thinks about his hands, his stance, his stride. It can be overwhelming. As a result, he tends to forget about the most important thing—*watching the baseball.*

The way a hitter handles adversity can be an important measure of the success he will have in his career. I try to give the slumping hitter something he can really believe in—one single thing that he can return to in those most trying times. Nine times out of ten, a guy in a slump is doing something different with his head. So I tell him to forget about everything except keeping his head down. Once you get him doing that, you've almost won the battle. His concentration improves, his intensity improves, and his confidence begins to return. The negative feelings that have been enveloping him at the plate begin to dissipate. A little positive thinking creeps in, because he believes he's got a chance again. That's the ticket out of a slump.

One sure way to stay in a slump is to go around the dugout listening to everyone's advice. One guy says this; another says the opposite. They're just relaying what works for them. That doesn't mean it will work for the guy in the slump. He shouldn't be adopting the habits of other hitters. He should be rediscovering his own best hitting habits by concentrating on the basics that worked for him in the past.

Slumps are funny things. Even the best hitters occasionally have periods when they go wrong. For a hitter like Wade Boggs it may last only two or three games. But for him, that's hard to handle. It's like somebody else going a week without a hit. Get into a slump, and the whole world seems to be operating against you. Suddenly, you're not seeing any 3 and 1 counts, only 0 and 2. The pitchers are hitting the corners with their nastiest pitches, and every ball you hit decently is right at someone. The guys who make it in this game are the ones who go out and do something about that slump. They don't just stand around feeling sorry for themselves; they concentrate and make adjustments.

The great Ted Williams—and he had very few serious slumps in his career—told me that when things were going wrong, he'd try to drive everything right back at the pitcher. This, from the greatest pull hitter of all time. But he knew that to break out of a slump, you have to concentrate on making one thing work. The difference between a good year and a great year, or a good year and a bad year, is how you handle slumps. Everybody has slumps. The great hitters don't have prolonged slumps.

Great hitters have their own personalities, but there is a common denominator. They're in control of their emotions all the time. They don't get too excited or high when things are going well. They don't get too far down in the dumps when they're going badly. They stay somewhere in the middle and sustains the same disciplined attitude and approach through good times and bad. That may sound funny. But just as a lot of hitters can't handle a slump, and thus unnecessarily prolong it, some hitters can't handle the good times. They get too keyed up and lose that essential concentration.

This is not as emotional a game as, say, football. It's not the kind of game where you spike the ball in the end zone. Sure, hit a game-winning homer to end the World Series and you can dance around the basepaths all you want. But day in, day out, you have to keep a rein on your emotions. You have to keep yourself on an even keel. Your body and mind have to be under control.

Boggs calls the state he's in a "cocoon." He's oblivious to everything outside him. Henry Aaron was the same way. Every time at the plate, he acted in a similar manner; it didn't matter if he hit a home run or struck out with the bases loaded. He never threw his helmet; he'd take it off and place it back in the rack. He had unbelievable control of his emotions. What an asset that is in a great ballplayer. With many good hitters, you'd like to put blinders on them, like racehorses, so they wouldn't get distracted by everything around them.

Baseball is a unique and wonderful game. It takes enormous physical skill to be a great hitter. But never underestimate the other attributes it takes to make a great ballplayer—heart and head. Physical tools aren't enough. Watch Wade Boggs, Don Mattingly, Mike Schmidt, Dwight Evans, George Brett, or Tim Raines. What they all share is a fabulous discipline and mental approach to the game. Together with their obvious physical skills, that sets them above the rest.

Good luck, and good hitting!

Photographing the Swing Sequence

The successful sequence photographs of Walter Hriniak's swing posed unusual problems, which were solved by Charles Miller, a high-speed photography expert at Massachusetts Institute of Technology. The task was to separate the fast, fluid motion of the swing into dozens of frames in which the bat, the ball, and the batter are sharp.

Mr. Miller's solution was to construct a special shutterless camera and to combine it with three special strobes. The camera is a modification of a shutterless, 35mm Fairchild radar recording camera, which can hold 100-foot rolls of film. An adjustable, regulated-speed motor pulls the film past the lens continuously, rather than intermittently. To freeze the motion of the bat, ball, and body, Mr. Miller used the 25-millionths-of-a-second flashes of three EG & G type 553 strobes. The flashes provided enough light to capture 60 images per second. To insure even illumination, Miller pointed the lamps toward the front, side, and top of Hriniak's body.

Photo Credits

Page 1: Peter Travers; page 3: Courtesy of the Boston Red Sox; page 5: Henry Horenstein; page 6: National Baseball Library, Cooperstown, NY; page 7: Courtesy of the Herman Seid collection; page 8: Walter Hriniak collection; page 10-11: Henry Horenstein; page 15: Courtesy of John Carroll; page 18: Courtesy of the Boston Red Sox; page 19: (top left): Henry Horenstein; (top right): Courtesy of the Boston Red Sox; (bottom left and right): Peter Travers; page 20 (top left): Henry Horenstein; (top right): Courtesy of the Boston Red Sox; (bottom left): Henry Horenstein; (bottom right): Peter Travers; page 21 (top left): Henry Horenstein; (top right and bottom left): Peter Travers; (bottom right): Courtesy of the Boston Red Sox; page 23: Henry Horenstein; page 25: National Baseball Library; page 27: Henry Horenstein; page 28-29: National Baseball Library; page 31: Henry Horenstein; page 32: Charles Miller; page 36 (top and bottom left and bottom right): Henry Horenstein; (top right): Courtesy of the Boston Red Sox; page 39: Henry Horenstein; page 40: Charles Miller; pages 42-43: (all photos): Henry Horenstein; page 45 (both photos): Henry Horenstein; page 47: Henry Horenstein; page 48: Charles Miller; page 50: Peter Travers; pages 52-53 (all photos): Henry Horenstein; page 55: Henry Horenstein; page 57-58: Charles Miller; page 59-60 (all photos): Henry Horenstein; page 61: (top left): Louis Requena; (top right): Henry Horenstein; (bottom left and right); Courtesy of the Boston Red Sox; pages 64-66: Charles Miller; page 68 (left): Henry Horenstein; (right): Courtesy of the Boston Red Sox; page 69 (top left): National Baseball Library; (top right): Courtesy of the Kansas City Royals; (bottom right): Courtesy of the Minnesota Twins; pages 72-78: Charles Miller; pages 79-85: Henry Horenstein; page 87: Louis Requena; page 91: (left and middle): Henry Horenstein; (right): Peter Travers; page 93: Henry Horenstein; page 97: Courtesy of the Boston Red Sox; page 101: Henry Horenstein; page 103: Henry Horenstein; page 104: Peter Travers; page 107: Peter Travers; page 109 (both photos): Peter Travers; page 110: (left): Henry Horenstein; (right): Peter Travers; pages 111-113: Peter Travers; page 114: Henry Horenstein; page 115: Courtesy of the California Angels; page 116: Courtesy of the Boston Red Sox; page 117: Henry Horenstein